Brian,

With best wishes!

Sanjay

Praise for *Fewer, Bigger, Bolder*

In *Fewer, Bigger, Bolder,* authors Mohanbir Sawhney and Sanjay Khosla challenge basic business assumptions and provide striking, counterintuitive ideas for winning high and sustainable revenue. They provide convincing case examples, and I expect this book to spark a major overhaul of business strategy thinking.
>—Philip Kotler, S.C. Johnson & Son Professor of International Marketing, Kellogg School of Management; author of *Market Your Way to Growth: 8 Ways to Win*

Outstanding practical insights bringing together years of front-line business experience with academic research. Provides a powerful formula for driving success in any business.
>—Vijay Govindarajan, Coxe Distinguished Professor at Tuck at Dartmouth and author of *New York Times* and *Wall Stree Journal* bestseller *Reverse Innovation*

Writing with genuine concern, passion for leadership, and uncanny insight, Sanjay Khosla and Mohanbir Sawhney delve into the complicated subject of business growth in *Fewer, Bigger, Bolder.* This is a must-read for all those who want to grow their businesses successfully with purpose!
>—Marshall Goldsmith, author or editor of thirty-four books including the global bestsellers *MOJO* and *What Got You Here Won't Get You There.*

Sanjay Khosla and Mohanbir Sawhney have succinctly and powerfully created a strategy for focus. It is a fascinating read and a guidebook for anyone competing in 2014 and beyond. Applying the authors' lessons will translate into profitable growth, competitive advantage, and bankable investments. They use their fifty-plus combined years of global experience to create a bible for management.
>—Michael Silverstein, senior partner, The Boston Consulting Group; co-author of *The $10 Trillion Prize*

If you're looking for pragmatic advice, profound focus, and exquisitely simple ideas, read this book. Sanjay Khosla's and Mohanbir Sawhney's wisdom is based on years of practical experience and success in growing businesses in the most competitive markets. They provide a true "how to" guide to getting it done.

—Shelly Lazarus, chairman emeritus, Ogilvy and Mather

A very insightful and practical guide to getting to growth that counts by simplifying your business, focusing where you can win and avoiding the "seduction of more." The ideas in the book really resonated with me. An essential read for growth leaders!

—Diane H. Gulyas, president, DuPont Performance Polymers, E. I. du Pont de Nemours and Company

Scale and scalability are important, but Mohanbir Sawhney and Sanjay Khosla challenge the corporate world's relentless drive for growth. Instead, they encourage readers to consider an approach they've honed over many years: stick to business essentials, be integrated and clear and simple in purpose and develop sustainable advantage. Their thesis chimes closely with the issues and opportunities faced in my daily work. *Fewer, Bigger, Bolder* is a thoughtful and action-provoking read.

—Rita Griffin, COO, BP Lubricants and CMO, BP Group

FEWER,
BIGGER,
BOLDER

FEWER, BIGGER, BOLDER

FROM MINDLESS EXPANSION TO FOCUSED GROWTH

SANJAY KHOSLA
AND
MOHANBIR SAWHNEY
WITH RICHARD BABCOCK

PORTFOLIO / PENGUIN

PORTFOLIO / PENGUIN
Published by the Penguin Group
Penguin Group (USA) LLC
375 Hudson Street
New York, New York 10014

USA I Canada I UK I Ireland I Australia I New Zealand I India I South Africa I China
penguin.com
A Penguin Random House Company

First published by Portfolio / Penguin, a member of Penguin Group (USA) LLC, 2014

LIBRARY OF CONGRESS CATALOGING-IN-PUBLICATION DATA
Khosla, Sanjay.
  Fewer, bigger, bolder : from mindless expansion of focused growth / Sanjay Khosla,
Mohanbir Sawhney.
    pages cm
Includes index.
  ISBN 978-1-59184-605-5 (hardback)
  ISBN 978-1-59184-760-1 (international edition)
  1. Corporations—Growth.   2. Success in business.   3. Management.   4. Strategic
planning.   I. Sawhney, Mohanbir S.   II. Title.
  HD2746.K47 2014
  658.4'063—dc23

                                                              2014004341

Printed in the United States of America
10 9 8 7 6 5 4 3 2

Set in Sabon LT Std
Designed by Alissa Rose Theodor

To Neelu, Namita, and Nikhil, my three Ns—who are my greatest strengths and help me focus on what really matters.

—*Sanjay Khosla*

To my strongest supporters—my mother, Kuldeep, who can see no wrong in my flaws, and my children, Asha and Bundev, who may someday finally figure out what Dad does for a living.

—*Mohanbir Sawhney*

FOREWORD

IRENE ROSENFELD

CHAIRMAN AND CEO, MONDELĒZ INTERNATIONAL

(Former Chairman and CEO, Kraft Foods, Inc.)

This is a smart, practical book about how to bring a business—any business—to sustained success. That's how most people will read it, and they will gain from it. But to me, this book will always be about that beloved cookie, the Oreo.

When Sanjay Khosla joined Kraft Foods in 2007, one of his first big challenges was what to do about Oreo. The cookie was coming up on its centennial celebration in the United States, where it had reigned for decades as one of America's favorite treats, known for the signature "twist, lick, dunk" ritual. But despite repeated, expensive efforts, Kraft Foods had been unable to interest consumers outside the United States in the iconic cookie. The frustration at Kraft Foods was palpable—families around the world were spending more money and opening up to foreign tastes and products, and, still, they didn't seem to give a whit for this classic cookie.

Enter Sanjay and his disciplined, innovative system for getting on track. Oreo blossomed into one of the most popular cookies around the world, an enormous hit for Kraft Foods and a billion-dollar brand in developing markets, where revenues quintupled in just five years. I won't give away the steps that led to this transformation—Sanjay and Northwestern professor Mohanbir Sawhney set them out carefully in the pages that follow. But I can attest to the fact that the Oreo story is an apt metaphor for Focus7, the framework that the authors describe in this book, a formula for growth that's both profitable and sustainable. The point is to drive a Virtuous Cycle of Growth, which is a concept Sanjay developed and championed over the years.

As the name implies, Focus7 starts with focus—focusing on what works. And "focus" is a word Sanjay repeated around Kraft Foods like a mantra. It's one of those words that comes up so often that they're easy to overlook or disregard—right, focus, now let's get on with our strategy meeting. But when a business or organization genuinely applies focus as a guiding principle under a carefully managed system, the results can be remarkable.

Sanjay and Professor Sawhney bring a unique combination of experiences to the table—Sanjay as a business executive, Professor Sawhney as an academic and consultant. In *Fewer, Bigger, Bolder* they explain their system, using language that's precise and accessible, and drawing on research from a number of companies around the world.

I'm confident this book will take its place in the library alongside the finest books on management—a classic, in its own way, just like the Oreo.

CONTENTS

XI

CONTENTS

INTRODUCTION

The demand is vital, implacable, and endlessly daunting: Grow. Every business has to grow. When it stops growing, it starts to wither. Even in the best of times, the demand presses. Just keeping up with inflation requires growth. And though cutting costs can buy you profits for a while, you can't shrink your way to greatness.

Sure, globalization and the digital revolution provide rich, exciting opportunities. But for all their potential benefits— political and economic—they've also added uncertainty to the marketplace with a force that's probably unprecedented in our lifetimes. Globalization has disrupted the pace of business and upended many of its traditional assumptions. And digitalization magnifies globalization's impact. The instant spread of information pressures everyone in the marketplace. Only the doomed plug along inside a bubble of complacency. New rivals, new products, and new challenges keep entering the game.

Add to this mix Wall Street's incessant demands for short-term results, and the question besets everyone from the CEO to business unit leaders to founders of start-up companies: How do we grow this business?

The question contains a trap. As we will show in this book,

too often the answer that comes back is: Find revenues wherever you can. As one CEO put it to Mohan: "We never met a revenue dollar we didn't like." The search for revenues leads to the usual roster of initiatives: Introduce new products, push into new markets, acquire new customers, and buy companies. All of these efforts seem to make sense in the noble pursuit of growth.

Too often, though, the net results of this frantic activity are disappointing. In our research, as we talked to many executives across industries around the world, we heard consistent refrains: "We are doing too much." "We are stretched too thin." "We are drowning in routine." "We have become too complex."

The fact is, when it comes to growing revenues, a dollar is not a dollar is not a dollar. In that realm, not all dollars are equal. Sure, the top line may have grown from $50 million to $80 million in the last three years, but what is the *quality* of those revenues? Quality revenues are profitable and sustainable. They promise ongoing growth that builds on itself.

Getting to the point of quality growth is the endgame—the point where your business outpaces the competition and your bottom line grows faster than your top line. And it's possible to do. Take a look at the recent experience of Kraft Foods, where Sanjay worked from 2007 to 2013. By 2006, Kraft's China venture was pouring money into a vast, bottomless hole. The company had spent two decades and untold dollars pursuing the enticing possibility of "a billion Chinese, therefore billions in sales." But Kraft was doing little more than chasing a mirage. Though investments backed a spreading smorgasbord of brands and projects, revenues limped in at less than $150 million annually. Kraft China was actually losing money. Worse, the venture had no hope of making money because it did not have a sustainable business model.

Why was this happening? Kraft enjoyed a stable of strong products, from Oreo cookies to Kraft Macaroni & Cheese to Planters peanuts. In the United States, Kraft was by far the number-one food company. But the Chinese consumer hardly seemed interested. For example, the Oreo—royalty among cookies in the American market—struggled in China. In a decade of effort, Kraft leadership had spawned countless initiatives to rally the Chinese business, but the projects just seemed to produce more fruitless activity. The situation was exhausting and unnerving for everyone involved. "The business was stuck in a vicious cycle," recalls Lorna Davis, who took over in 2007 as business leader for Kraft China, "and we knew that expanding our current business model was not going to work."

At the time, China wasn't the only trouble spot in Kraft's international operations. The company's ventures in markets around the world were sprawling and disjointed. Kraft was planting flags in countries all over the globe with lots of frenetic activity, little coordination, and not much to show for the effort. The company was expanding—that's what enterprising businesses do, right? But the business models for the new ventures lacked the discipline to provide significant payoffs—they were part of a wave of mindless expansion. Even in areas where revenues were growing, the margins remained anemic and the prognosis offered little promise. Something radical had to be done.

The turnaround for Kraft Developing Markets, which had recently hired Sanjay as president, came by way of a bold plan that contradicts the expansionist gospel of today. The plan represents the system we lay out in this book, and it's based on a handful of key principles:

- Do less. Make fewer bets but make them bigger. Focus where you can win.
- Be bold. Distort resources to focus them on the highest-potential initiatives.
- Simplify and keep costs low. Cut complexity from your plans, your organization, and your processes.
- Execute! Keep testing, learning, and adjusting.
- Unleash people. Bet on people by giving them disproportionate resources and authority.

We will follow Kraft's experience throughout this book, but here, in brief, is how the process unfolded: In early 2007 the company organized workshops of key personnel and knowledgeable outsiders. The brief was simple: Figure out what's working and what has the potential to grow. Take the money you've been spreading throughout an overstuffed portfolio and concentrate it behind the handful of initiatives that have momentum, good margins, and the size to make a difference. And do it quickly, without endless deadly meetings and mountains of numbing memos.

Within months, Kraft Developing Markets kicked off a

strategy that it labeled 5-10-10. From a portfolio featuring dozens of categories of products, more than 150 brands, and over sixty countries, the business would concentrate on five strong categories, ten power brands, and ten key markets. The new approach narrowed the company's attention and targeted resources—it allowed the company to make a few big bets. Equally important, it provided a guide for making the selective cuts to fund those bets and a blueprint on where to simplify a baggy operation. Finally, because 5-10-10 wasn't simply handed down from on high, but was created by a team, the strategy brought a sense of ownership and alignment to Kraft's widely dispersed regional leaders and allowed them to push responsibility for making key decisions down to the local level, where people knew the culture and the market.

The results speak for themselves. Within six years, the developing markets division soared from $5 billion in revenues to $16 billion, with double-digit organic growth. And that was *bankable* growth, as profitability shot up 50 percent, along with a significant improvement in cash flow.

China, that longtime money pit, completely turned around. By the end of 2012, Kraft's revenues in China exceeded $1 billion, with healthy margins and a model that anticipates continued profitable growth.

And as for Oreo—it got picked as one of the ten power brands and turned into one of those big bets. In a dramatic, come-from-behind story, the Oreo business grew from $200 million outside North America in 2006 to more than $1 billion in 2012—and with healthy margins. The cookie now ranks number one in China. Whereas a few years ago Kraft was considering giving up on Oreo there, ex-NBA star Yao Ming has taught his countrymen the signature Oreo move: twist, lick, dunk.

Tang, another Kraft 5-10-10 power brand, went from $500 million in developing markets in 2006—a level it had taken almost half a century to reach—to more than $1 billion in 2012.

The problems Kraft faced a decade ago around the globe echo problems that crop up constantly throughout the business world, whether the operation is a sprawling multinational or a local stalwart, a global giant or a lean start-up. Even divisions within larger companies often go astray. The trouble usually comes from trying to do too much in the search for growth.

We offer a different approach. In our view, the opposite of mindless expansion is *sustainable growth*—that is, growth that continues and builds on itself. Sustainable growth is growth that you can maintain without twisting yourself into a pretzel each quarter to make your numbers; growth that produces decent margins; growth that makes organization charts subservient to profits and not the other way around; growth that favors simplicity over complexity.

Sustainable growth is not something you get to overnight. It is a journey that requires continuing effort. We hope this book serves as a GPS, so to speak, to guide you along the way. A GPS is more than a map. A map provides the overall view of the territory—the lay of the land, the towns and cities, the roads, the lakes, the landmarks. A GPS, in contrast, tells you how to get someplace. You type in the destination, and it gives turn-by-turn directions, providing alternative routes when necessary and warning about roadblocks and detours. Too many business strategy books are like maps—they tell you the lay of the land but leave you to your own devices to navigate your way to the destination. This book is about execution. We will show you *how* to get to sustainable growth. And when you get there, we will show you how to stay there. Luck is a critical factor of success, but our disciplined yet agile approach helps you be lucky.

We call our framework Focus7, because it includes seven steps and because the journey to sustained growth almost always begins with focus. By that we mean isolating priorities—the facets of the business that really work, that can bring healthy, continuing profits—and then being disciplined, even ruthless, in steering resources toward those priorities. That word *focus* gets tossed around regularly, in business and almost everywhere else. But to borrow from the classic remark about the weather: Everybody talks about focus and nobody does anything about it. If you are going to get to sustainable growth, however, you are going to have to go through the hard exercise of focusing, and in the first two chapters, we'll show you some examples of focused and nonfocused companies to illustrate our point.

In addition to our extensive research, Focus7 reflects our own disparate journeys through a combined total of more than half a century in business. We have taken different paths but have arrived at very similar conclusions about the pursuit of sustainable growth. On the one hand—through Sanjay—we have had extensive practical experience in the packaged goods business and in global markets, dealing every day with the long- and short-term issues presented in running a company. On the other hand—through Mohan—we have the broader perspective offered by global consulting and academic research. Both of us have also worked with start-ups and across industries. We have complemented this experience with extensive interviews with executives from a wide variety of companies and industries. The Focus7 framework applies independently of what function you are in or level in the organization.

Following through on our prescription requires both firmness and flexibility, and we'll talk about that. At a number of points, our approach contradicts conventional wisdom—it takes confidence and steady nerves to move forward, and we'll walk you through the agenda. We provide case studies, many drawn from Sanjay's experience applying Focus7 at Kraft and before that at Fonterra Brands, a global dairy cooperative, and at Unilever's Lipton Tea and Unilever's Home and Personal Care Division. All operations enjoyed outstanding results. Other case studies rely on Mohan's consulting work and research, with large companies such as Hyatt, Microsoft, Cisco, and AT&T, as well as with mid-market companies and start-ups, where he has served as board member or adviser.

We are also happy to acknowledge that we have made plenty of mistakes along the way, and we will pass on whatever wisdom we have gained from those hard lessons.

As we said, Focus7's goal is to elevate a business to a position where it is growing profitably and its growth continues in a self-sustaining cycle. We call that achieving a Virtuous Cycle of Growth. Reaching the Virtuous Cycle doesn't mean a business leader can sit back and relax. Keeping the cycle rolling and dealing with unexpected bumps requires the continued reliance on many of the actions described in Focus7. But the Virtuous Cycle offers a proven formula for ongoing success.

Here's how we lay out our framework in the pages that follow: In chapter 1, we show how easy it is to fall into the trap of confusing quantity with quality, following seemingly good logic into expansion that's unproductive and that burdens the organization with strangling layers of complexity. Chapter 2 illustrates the advantages of a company with focus and recounts the discipline of mind and willingness to confront orthodoxies often required to stay on track.

Our Focus7 framework involves seven carefully choreographed steps, and we cover them in chapters 3 to 9.

Chapter 3: Discovery—Smart growth starts with insights that can be turned into opportunities to be scaled up and developed. Serendipity plays a role here, but we show you how to look systematically through analytic channels to generate promising insights. A key part of the discovery process is aligning leadership behind potential new initiatives—spreading ownership, so to speak—using tools like carefully orchestrated workshops that bring top managers into the discovery process.

Chapter 4: Strategy—The insights generated in step 1 need to be synthesized and prioritized. We explain how to examine them through various dimensions of the business—products, platforms, markets, customer segments, distribution channels, and so on. Looking through these dimensions—lenses, we call them—brings discipline to opportunity analysis and helps spotlight the big bets that will be the driving force of the company's growth. Each promising initiative should be measured by what we call the Three *Ms*—Momentum, Margin, and Materiality. The narrowed focus allows you to concentrate resources on areas where you have the best chance of winning.

Chapter 5: Rallying Cry—To take the strategy beyond the boardroom and into the fields and factories, companies need to articulate a clear and simple rallying cry, something to serve as a powerful aligning and motivating force. Strategies can be complex, but they need to be communicated with radical simplicity—and not necessarily in words. Rallying cries can be communicated through slogans, acronyms, pictures, or even colors. In this chapter, we lead you through the creative process of finding the best rallying cry to communicate your strategy and show how the tone set can add a unique culture to the organization.

Chapter 6: People—Ultimately, the success of a company entails not just betting on fresh opportunities, but betting on key people—wagering that they have the smarts, the passion, and the energy to transform a business. And diversity and teamwork can be a significant competitive advantage. In moving forward, it's absolutely necessary to have the right people in place.

Once they are in place, your key people need to have wide freedom to operate within the parameters of the strategy. That means distorting resources—shifting money, manpower, and effort from slower areas of the business and allocating them disproportionately to the focus initiatives. Occasionally, this reallocation unlocks all the usual constraints, including the budget. We will show how, under the right circumstances, teams should be given daunting targets, but almost unlimited resources. In our experience, they almost always rise to the challenge responsibly, and outcomes far exceed expectations.

Chapter 7: Execution—This is the most important step in the journey, and it is also the most difficult. Too often, fresh initiatives get lost in the maze of disparate ventures and blurred lines of authority. Yet there are practical ways to simplify the operation, which we discuss. Cost cutting comes into play here, and we show how to benchmark internally and externally to find the cuts to fuel growth. In moving forward, you are always test-ing and learning, scaling up when the results support it.

Chapter 8: Organization—Fresh, innovative opportunities rarely fall within the established lines of a company's organi-zation—the silos of function, geography, and business unit. To create sustainable growth, you need to build an opportunity-focused company, one that relies on collaborative networks that cross the usual borders and concentrate on a few selected projects. Like breaking the boundaries of budgets, this some-times requires a confrontation with orthodoxy. But the shift-ing, expanding global marketplace and the Internet-fueled evolution of consumer tastes require new shapes and alliances.

We also devote space in this chapter to the concept we call Going Glocal—finding the balance between a company's global resources and its local expertise. Many companies working in-ternationally aim too far one way or the other—they are mind-lessly global or hopelessly local. We offer the analysis to find the right balance.

Chapter 9: Metrics—As the focusing process gets under way, it's important to measure the right things the right way. The scorecard should relate directly to the goals, which may change in different stages of an initiative's growth. And like everything else in this framework, simplicity is crucial—leaders should monitor just a few key metrics. We outline the principles of monitoring by showing how to choose a few good metrics to track performance.

Once we have described the steps of Focus7, in chapter 10 we point out some of the pitfalls in implementing our framework and suggest ways to avoid trouble. Finally, in chapter 11 we walk through the Virtuous Cycle of Growth, in which revenues steadily increase and costs come down.

As you will see, our emphasis is determinedly forward looking. We think too many companies spend too much time chewing over the past, analyzing past initiatives, discussing what has happened rather than moving ahead with action. Our bias toward action is summed up well by the Hindi phrase *Karna Kya Hai?* (often shortened to KKH), which can loosely be translated as *"So what do we do now?"* That's the point. The past has already happened, it's already with us. Now we need to move on. What do we do?

We should emphasize that Focus7 is not designed for a one-time intervention—it's not another management scheme to be imposed on a weary workforce and then abandoned when a new leadership team takes over. Our program requires perseverance, but it provides a methodology that can be used repeatedly and in a range of contexts. It teaches a discipline of mind that advances skills throughout the company. Note also that Focus7 is not intended to produce short-term jumps in revenues or profits. The idea is to create a strategic model that continues to pay off over time.

None of this falls into place automatically. We have been refining Focus7 for years, and when it's deployed, leaders need to stay both controlled and flexible. We have framed the process here as sequential steps, but some leapfrogging up and back is inevitable. This is an *entrepreneurial* approach—implanting the ongoing process is a key to succeeding.

Attaining sustainable growth doesn't entail advanced physics, however. The process we describe essentially tracks how smart, effective people manage in all walks of life. Focus7 is simply a market-tested framework to help lead an organization to the promised land. And we think the process invites exploration, innovation, even fun. It discourages hierarchical thinking in favor of getting the news from the front lines of action and giving authority to the people actually on the ground. It promotes the thrill of discovery and the challenge of testing ideas. It encourages collaboration and emphasizes the promising future, not the failed past. And above all, of course, it instills a culture of winning and offers the pleasure of seeing great results roll in.

CHAPTER 1

THE SEDUCTION OF MORE

The quest for growth leads companies to expand into new markets, new product categories, new geographies, and new customer segments. Each move seems logical when made, but expansion without focus often leads only to disappointment. Capabilities get stretched beyond the company's comfort zone. Complexity increases faster than revenues. Complications arise with acquired businesses. After meandering for years in pursuit of expansion, companies retreat to refocus on their core. Many business leaders have confessed to us in private: It seemed like a good idea at the time, but I wish we had been more mindful.

Consider the foray into the consumer market of Cisco Systems, the hugely successful provider of networking equipment. Cisco had survived a bumpy ride after the dot-com bust that began in 2000 and recovered strongly under John Chambers, the widely admired long-term CEO. But by 2007, the company was feeling new pressure to grow revenues, and Chambers and his team began to succumb to the pressures of expansion. The logic seemed impeccable—technology was spreading explosively, the consumer market was mushrooming, and opportunities in the "consumerization of technology" beckoned. In 2010, at the annual weeklong Cisco Live conference for networking and communication professionals, Chambers proudly told a vast audience of guests in Las Vegas that Cisco had introduced four hundred new products in the last year. More than thirty initiatives came in what the company called adjacencies—markets and products that seemed close to current Cisco businesses.

Probably nothing symbolized the company's changing vision more than its pursuit of the Flip, the popular and handy little camcorder. Since its founding in 1984, Cisco had kept its eyes trained on business markets, but in 2009 Cisco paid $590 million to buy Pure Digital, the Flip's maker—a leap into consumer products. Why not? The whole world was getting into the consumer market, spurred by Apple's phenomenal success and by the drive to put a device—preferably several—in the hands of just about everyone. How was Cisco going to keep up if it was nothing more than a "plumber" of the technology world, as Chambers once put it?

Just two years later, Cisco shut down its Flip division. Though the camera continued to sell well, the margins were relatively low and the device faced growing competition from smartphones. Chambers said the Flip's demise was part of an effort to bring operations back in line with Cisco's core networking business.

The Flip was only a tiny piece of the giant Cisco, but the camera's fate was the tip of a very large iceberg. Between the time the company announced Pure Digital's acquisition on March 19, 2009, and the announcement of the Flip's shutdown on April 12, 2011, Cisco's margins slipped and net income was uneven. The company lost share in its core routing and switching markets as it expanded aggressively into dozens of adjacent markets, including high-end videoconferencing, energy-management gear, and consumer products. As Zeus Kerravala of the Yankee Group told *Network World* in February 2011, "Why wouldn't they stick to the stuff they do well and move into 10 markets instead of 30?"

After several quarters of disappointing results and a 30 percent fall in Cisco's stock price from April 2010 to April 2011 (even as the NASDAQ rose 15 percent), Chambers got the message. In April 2011, he announced that Cisco would "address with surgical precision what we need to fix in our portfolio." He outlined a streamlined strategy focused on a handful of key areas, including Cisco's core networking business as well as video, collaboration, and data-center technology. He also announced that Cisco would simplify its bloated and overly complex organization, which had ended up confusing its employees and disappointing its investors. After flirting disastrously with mindless expansion, Cisco has rediscovered the power of focus.

Cisco's experience suggests how seemingly logical growth moves can have unintended consequences. Carlos Dominguez, a senior vice president at Cisco, told Mohan in an interview, "People in big companies are not stupid. The senior managers at Cisco are really brilliant people. They've got the right heart, they've got the right desire. They're operating in the best interests of customers and shareholders. Each move Cisco made was a logical evolution of where we needed to go into adjacent markets. But every time you respond to issues that come up in the market by developing new products, expanding into adjacent businesses, or making acquisitions, you end up with very complex organizations. It sneaks up on you. Eventually, you have to prioritize. You have to ask: What are the things that made us what we are? What are we good at? What are the essential things we want to do? And you move from all of these opportunities into a very, very finite set of things that you're going to do and you're going to do very well. And I think that's what we've done."

Cisco's experience is hardly isolated. Over the years and through various economic climates, companies have heedlessly turned to expansion—too often without a disciplined approach. The notion of quality gets confused with quantity. It can happen with a sprawling multinational, such as Hewlett-Packard, which is struggling to compete in everything from mobile devices to printers to business services, and it can afflict midsize companies, such as Skullcandy, which has introduced several hundred models of headphones. Even nascent technology start-ups can fall into the trap of chasing too many opportunities at the same time and losing focus before they have their first product. Whatever the situation, the mindless pursuit of growth usually results in stumbles from which it can take years to recover.

These unfocused expansions are very understandable, very human, in a sense. Logic underlies virtually all of them. Companies need to open new markets, launch new products, explore new businesses. Every extension usually brings some additional revenue, at least in the short term, so there's rarely a push back. In isolation, every opportunity looks good. And from the vantage point of a product manager or a business unit leader looking at his or her silo, every new product or market seems promising. But expansion can become addictive, and after a while companies tend to binge like junkies on product variants, brands, acquisitions, and new markets.

We call this syndrome the Seduction of More. The siren song can take a variety of forms. Sometimes it taps into a basic imperative to get bigger, as leaders are pressured by investors to grow the top line. Other times, the herd mentality takes over—everyone else is building a tablet or everyone else is moving into India or China, hence, we should, too. Sometimes ego is the driving force—when it comes to acquisitions, for example. Closing a deal and acquiring something becomes a payoff in itself.

Even the best-run companies aren't immune to the seduction. Consider the story of Illinois Tool Works (ITW), a one-hundred-year-old conglomerate. Founded in 1912, ITW grew to nearly $18 billion in annual revenues by 2012 by acquiring hundreds of small companies over several decades. This acquisition binge resulted in a sprawling confederation of 850 autonomous businesses operating in fifty-eight countries. Each unit brought in an average of less than $30 million in revenues.

In 2012, the company operated seven primary business segments and an additional "miscellaneous" segment. A company video proudly noted, "If it's wrapped, scrapped, fastened, or welded; built, connected, balanced, or sliced; decorated, packaged, labeled, or protected, chances are Illinois Tool Works is behind it."

For the transportation industry, ITW makes components, fasteners, fluids, and polymers. For industrial packaging, it manufactures steel, plastic, and paper products used for building, shipping, and protecting goods in transport. The power systems and electronics unit manufactures power conversion and electronics. The food equipment segment builds commercial food equipment. In construction products, ITW builds tools, fasteners, and other construction products. The polymers and fluids unit manufactures adhesives, sealants, lubricants, and other fluids. The decorative services unit manufactures items such as countertops and flooring.

For years, this decentralized conglomerate produced steady growth in revenues and profits. But in the aftermath of the 2008 recession, ITW's growth began to sputter, and the company struggled to manage its scattershot portfolio. In its one hundredth year, ITW announced a major shift in strategy that embraces focus. The company would pare down its business portfolio from 850 units to between 120 and 150 units. ITW plans to divest up to 25 percent of the company's $18 billion in annual sales by shedding low-growth businesses and investing in those with higher growth prospects and the potential to differentiate. And the company is swearing off acquisitions for now, choosing instead to improve its execution. Sounding like a recovering growth addict, CEO E. Scott Santi commented, "If we can narrow our focus and create a company that can grow sales 5 percent to 7 percent a year organically, what's wrong with that? We needed to recalibrate how we think about growth."

That is our message. Companies need to rethink their assumptions about growth.

Globalization has intensified the Seduction of More—all those tempting markets in China, Brazil, India, Indonesia, and other parts of the developing world. The promise is almost irresistible. But the payoff—as Kraft discovered over the years in its China venture—is hardly a sure thing.

Even start-ups risk falling under the spell of More, often even before they have a product! For them, the problem usually manifests in an overabundance of seeming opportunities. Which direction to take? How to avoid chasing rabbits running in every direction across the field? Business is full of examples of scattered and struggling start-ups. Consider RealNetworks, Inc., a technology company in the digital software and media business. Founded by Rob Glaser, who'd amassed a fortune as an executive at Microsoft, the company began life in 1994 as a system for trading information about progressive politics. But after pioneering in digital audio and video with its RealPlayer system and becoming an investor favorite in the dot-com boom, RealNetworks never really settled on a core business. It acquired Rhapsody and ran a music store and a media subscription service, but eventually spun off the operation. It began creating and distributing online games. It developed a system, Unifi, for individuals to manage their assorted media from a variety of devices. It plays in the mobile phone field with ringtone services, among other things. A professional services unit offers technological support. And that just begins to pull from a cluttered and marked-up résumé. (With all that dashing around, RealNetworks actually let one rabbit run past without giving chase—Tony Fadell unsuccessfully tried to interest the company in a system for gathering music linked to a device for playing it. He later caught the attention of Apple, which eventually turned his ideas into the iPod.)

Given all the unproductive activity, it's hardly a surprise that RealNetworks has been through four CEOs in recent years (including founder Rob Glaser twice) and not done well. In hindsight, it seems obvious that companies like RealNetworks should pick their bets carefully and stick to their knitting. But this isn't easy to do when you are struggling to grow your revenues and customer base. Faced with these pressures and with investors breathing down your neck, no opportunity seems too trivial or too distracting to pursue. It requires enormous discipline to say no to the many rabbits that emerge from the woods.

UPSIDE-DOWN MARKETING

Companies eager to grow get desperate, and in their anxiety they return to the established patterns of behavior. A few years ago, Mohan was approached by a multinational technology company looking for ways to spark growth fast. The company wanted something that would pay off in twelve months. The request hardly made sense: Almost anything that adds growth requires you to do something new—enter a new market, build new products, target a new customer segment. Adding takes time.

On the other hand, deleting can happen in a blink. You can almost always stop doing something stupid faster than you can start something new. Mohan decided to approach the problem from the opposite direction and think: What should the company stop doing?

He put together a presentation—whimsically called "Upside-Down Marketing"—that turned business assumptions on their head. Where the marketing gospel preaches "acquire more customers," he said, no, fire the customers that are not profitable. The gospel says "launch more products." No, kill the products that are not producing profits and revenue. Add more brands. No, put your weight behind a few brands. Enter new markets. No, focus on the few markets where you can win and dominate.

This prescription echoes the principles of Focus7. The company liked the ideas, but implementation requires more than inspiration—it requires execution, and in this instance, the company fell short.

STRANGLED BY COMPLEXITY

Succumbing to the Seduction of More produces one almost sure-fire outcome: increased corporate complexity. Regardless of the nature of the business or the size of the operation, companies with unguided expansion tend to develop elaborate infrastructures—each new product extension gets its own teams for management, marketing, and distribution. More systems, more reports, more rules, more people. Complexity leaches into the operation.

Even a well-run company like Microsoft is a prime example. Mohan saw this firsthand a few years ago on a visit to the technology giant's sprawling Redmond, Washington, campus. He had been working with Microsoft for years, and he occasionally puzzled over the way the company's product extensions seemed to spring up like mushrooms after a rain. For example, almost every new Windows version had grown its own little infrastructure—adding up to more costs and complexity, often without commensurate returns.

So he asked a group of Microsoft executives a simple question: Can you tell me what customers should know about the difference between Windows XP Home and Windows XP Pro? They hemmed and hawed. Finally, someone came up with the key difference—Windows XP Pro allowed users to remotely log into their computers. This feature clearly did not make for an earth-shattering distinction. If company executives couldn't explain the reason why different versions of products exist, how are customers supposed to figure it out?

Complexity almost always strangles profits. Revenues grow linearly, and complexity grows nonlinearly. And the problem often doesn't make itself apparent until it's too late. It's like overeating—just as it takes fifteen minutes for the message that you are full to get from your stomach to your head, companies expand but suffer a delay in recognizing what is happening. By then, the corporate calories have piled up.

UNDERSTANDING COMPLEXITY

Before we show you how to deal with complexity, you need to understand how to measure it. By understanding the nature of the affliction, you can get a better handle on how far the cancer of complexity has progressed in your company. Here's a simple conceptual framework to help.

Any business can be defined along four key dimensions. Stated simply, a business makes *something* for *somebody* that it sells *somewhere* by operating *somehow*. The four key dimensions of the business are:

1. The WHAT: These are the *Offerings* that a company creates. They include the company's products, services, solutions, platforms, and brands.
2. The WHO: These are the *Customers* that a company serves directly or indirectly. These can be defined in terms of customer segments, customer accounts, or industries that the company serves.

3. The WHERE: These are the *Markets* that a company operates in. They include the domestic region as well as international markets.

4. The HOW: These are the *Operations* that the company owns in order to do business. They include the factories, distribution centers, supply chains, warehouses, and other physical facilities.

For example, consider a company like John Deere. In terms of *Offerings*, John Deere produces 201 distinct product lines, including dump trucks, gas barbecue grills, hand tools, garden tractors, riding mowers, and snow removal equipment. In terms of *Customers*, John Deere participates in nine distinct market segments, including agriculture, commercial, construction, sports, and residential markets. In terms of *Markets*, Deere operates in thirty countries around the world. And as for the *Operations*, Deere operates dozens of factories, multiple channels of distribution, and manages a complex network of suppliers and partners around the world.

These are the four dimensions on which the complexity of a company can be defined and measured. The dimensions of complexity are therefore:

Offering complexity: How many distinct products, variants, brands, and stock-keeping units (SKUs) does the company offer? Consider a large consumer packaged goods company. It may have five hundred brands, each of which may be sold in six sizes and a dozen forms or flavors. These in turn may have up to ten local variations. These quickly add up to more than

250,000 SKUs. The complexity of the offering increases with the proliferation of SKUs, driven by new flavors, new pack sizes, new formulations, new packaging forms, and new localized products in international markets.

Customer complexity: How diverse are the company's customers, measured in terms of distinct lines of business, vertical markets, industries served, and customer segments targeted? Do the customers span B2B (business to business) as well as B2C (business to consumer) segments? A large technology company may market its products and services to consumers, small businesses, midsize businesses, large enterprises, and public sector organizations. Within each of these market segments, there are a number of customer segments. In the enterprise markets, customers may include industries like retail, insurance, banking, telecommunications, packaged goods, and energy. The greater the diversity of customers, the more difficult it becomes to decide which products and services to offer to each customer segment, how to reach each customer segment effectively, and how to measure the profitability of each customer segment.

Market complexity: How many distinct countries or geographical markets does the company operate in? How diverse is its geographical footprint? A complex multinational may operate in scores of countries around the world. Each of these countries may in turn have a number of regions. It may have hundreds or thousands of physical offices across these regions and countries. Each geography and region needs a separate local management team, resources, and plans. Then there is the challenge of coordinating activities across regions and markets and deciding what to centralize versus decentralize.

Operations complexity: How complicated are the company's operations, in terms of the layers in its supply chain, number of manufacturing facilities, diversity of distribution channels, number and diversity of partnerships, number of acquisitions made by the company, and the diversity of its information technology (IT) systems? A large company may operate hundreds of factories around the world and it may market its products through a vast network of global distributors and retailers. The larger the number of factories and the larger the network of distribution operations, the more complex the management of operations becomes.

These dimensions of complexity do not add up. They multiply. The total complexity of a company's business is the product of its offering complexity, customer complexity, market complexity, and operations complexity. By relating these four dimensions to the company's revenues, you can get a sense of how complexity drags down earnings. For a simple measure of complexity, multiply the number of products, customers, markets, and operations entities in your business. Now divide your total revenues by this number. The lower the figure that results, the less efficient your company is at generating revenues. The summary point: Expansion is seductive, but it inevitably adds complexity. Further, this complexity grows faster than revenues do. As a result, complexity is the enemy of profitable growth.

How do you know if you've been seduced by More? Ask yourself the following diagnostic questions about your business:

- Have your recent new products been less profitable than those in the past?
- Are you scraping the bottom of the barrel in acquiring new customers?
- Have your most recent acquisitions reduced profit margins?
- Are those recent acquisitions contributing more headaches to the leadership team than revenue to the company?
- Has your top line been growing faster than your bottom line in recent quarters?
- Are your revenues per employee declining?
- Are your selling and administrative expenses creeping up as a percentage of revenues?
- Are the people in your company confused about the top priorities?
- Are you floundering in some of the geographical markets you have entered recently?
- Is your organization matrixed to the hilt with unclear lines of accountability?
- Are you seeing increasing employee attrition and decreasing employee morale?

If your answers tilt toward yes, you have probably succumbed. The time has come to focus.

CHAPTER 2

THE WISDOM OF LESS

Over the last decade or so, running an airline has been an unenviable task. Rocketing fuel prices, increased competition, weather disruptions, labor problems, increased regulation, security threats, delays in new aircraft deliveries—the litany of problems is never-ending. Airlines around the world, from Alitalia to Air India to American Airlines have swum in red ink, sometimes taking refuge in bankruptcy. Every now and then the situation improves for a while, but the overall story of airline profits has been grim. Yet, amid the turmoil, a few airlines have stood out with their sustained growth and profits, even through the global financial crisis. Let's look at two airlines that are poles apart in every way, yet tell the same story—the story of Winning Through Focus.

A passenger flying on Spirit Airlines typically starts by buying a ridiculously cheap ticket—often hundreds of dollars cheaper than anything offered by competing airlines. When the passenger arrives at the departure gate, he isn't likely to find a Spirit employee with the time or inclination to answer questions, though he is likely to find a line at the counter. If the passenger checks bags, he pays $30 or more for each. If he has a carry-on that won't fit under the seat, he will pay for that, too. Once on the plane, he'll sit in the seat Spirit assigned him—unless he paid to choose his own. In either case, he'll occupy one of the most cramped spaces of any commercial airline, with his knees probably pressing into the seat in front. He could pay extra for a slightly roomier ride, but there's no first class here. During the flight, a beer or a snack will cost him—even water comes at a price ($3). He won't watch a movie because the plane isn't equipped with viewing monitors for passengers, though he might entertain himself by looking at the assorted advertisements plastered on the overhead bins. The flight attendants—if he can summon one—have little time to coddle travelers. When he finally disembarks at his destination, he'll almost certainly exhale in relief at the conclusion of what countless travelers have pronounced one of the most miserable travel experiences they have ever endured. Yet, chances are he will come back and fly Spirit Airlines again, because he knows what he is getting, and he is willing to trade comfort and convenience for a low price.

A passenger flying Emirates also starts with a ticket, but it might cost $10,000 or more for first class, often thousands more than for a seat on competing airlines. If she lives near a major metropolitan area and she's a first-class or business-class passenger, she needn't fret about schlepping to the airport. A chauffeur-driven car will whisk her there. It's unlikely she'll find irksome, unattended lines at the gate, and, in any case, if she's one of those top-tier passengers, she'll wait in a full-service Emirates lounge and perhaps enjoy a carefully prepared meal. Was her departure from home hasty? She can take a shower here. In buying her ticket, she has chosen among three classes of accommodations—first class, business, and economy—and let's say she's bought a business-class ticket (because she's already showered in the lounge, she assumes she won't need to use one of the showers in the first-class cabin on many Emirates flights). She'll fly in a roomy seat that converts to a flat bed when necessary. If her back stiffens, her seat offers a soothing massage. Her personal entertainment system features more than 1,500 channels, and lovely champagne and wines complement the five-course meals. The alert attendants politely see to her comfort—fresh fruit, more champagne—and when she arrives at her destination another car waits to ferry her to her first stop, concluding an air journey that many travelers have ranked one of the finest they have ever encountered.

Aside from both being in the air travel business, Spirit and Emirates appear to have almost nothing in common. Spirit, headquartered in Miramar, Florida, uses its aggressively pared-down, à la carte operation to serve the domestic American and Caribbean markets. Emirates, based in Dubai, offers its premium service to long-haul international travelers. But while the industry has bounced through a period of almost unending recent turbulence, both companies have enjoyed remarkably consistent success. Spirit Airlines, which introduced its no-frills system in 2006 and went public in May 2011, has seen net income triple since 2008. Ancillary revenues make up a third of its income and are expected to continue to grow. From its modest founding in 1985, Emirates has grown into one of the largest airlines in the world and has suffered only one year when it didn't make a profit. It is consistently ranked one of the best carriers in terms of service as it grows aggressively into a top global brand.

Both companies have benefited from a number of factors and idiosyncrasies that have contributed to their overall success. However, each has thrived for one overriding reason: focus. While the legacy airlines have tried to be everything to everybody, Spirit's gaze has been fixed unwaveringly on offering cheap tickets and hitting up passengers for fees. Spirit CEO Ben Baldanza makes no apologies for the no-frills approach. "No one at McDonald's is worried they don't have the same product as Morton's Steakhouse," he recently told *Flightglobal*. "No one at the dollar store wants to be Nordstrom."

Emirates has never deviated from the pricey but elegant service that's a hallmark of its operation. "In the end, if you have a good product, you offer value for money," Emirates president Tim Clark told the same publication. "That's the most important thing. People value that notion. If you offer value for money, they'll keep coming back to you."

Several other companies illustrate a similar winning strategy— staying focused. IKEA made its niche with first-time home buyers who are price and style conscious. In its crowded field, Enterprise Rent-A-Car concentrates on the replacement car market— providing vehicles for local consumers whose family car is being repaired. The most successful American company of our time, Apple, famously features only a handful of products and brands, and its founder, Steve Jobs, repeated the word "focus" endlessly.

Start-ups also need focus. Segway stumbled trying to market its stand-up personal transportation machine to the mass consumer market as a new way for pedestrians to get around. But the company found enthusiastic buyers when narrowing its aim to professional groups, such as police departments and tour operators.

The principle holds true in global markets, too. Kraft turned around its floundering China venture with a focus strategy that emphasized a few chosen categories, brands, and markets.

These experiences illustrate a key point: Growth isn't about doing more, it's about doing things better. In fact, growth can come from doing less—by focusing your efforts, you can do a few things well. Focus begets simplicity in strategy and clarity in execution. Winemakers have learned that to improve the quality of their grapes and get the best yields, they need to prune their bushes. The same paradox applies to business. To grow, you must cut.

Even within companies, focus applies to all functions. Consider manufacturing. When Mohan worked for a watch company called Titan Watches in India in the 1980s, the company realized it had a problem in its factory. Titan offered hundreds of watch models catering to all segments, styles, and price points in the market. A few models were the bread and butter aimed at the mass market. Those models sold tens of thousands of units every year, but brought in slim margins. At the other extreme came the complex and expensive models aimed at the high end. They sold a few hundred units, but delivered high profit margins. Titan realized that it could not manufacture the mass-market watches the same way as the high-end watches, so the company created two factories within the factory. One was the mass production line. It was highly automated and had low production costs per watch, but low flexibility, because it rarely needed to change from making one model to another. The other production line was the job shop—designed to produce complicated and delicate watches using skilled manual labor. The job shop was optimized for flexibility, but the production cost was much higher per watch. In all, Titan had created focused factories—one designed for mass, low-cost production and another for low-volume, complex production. By bringing focus to manufacturing, Titan was able to satisfy both ends of its market.

The same logic applies to marketing decisions, such as branding. The smartphone business makes a good case in point: Samsung and Apple stand head and shoulders above the competition. What do the two companies have in common? Both have a focused brand strategy. Apple makes the iPhone. Period. It has no other brand. You can get it in different memory capacities and with different networking capabilities, but it is still called the iPhone. Samsung has followed the same strategy in recent years. After initially expanding its brand portfolio—with the BlackJack, the Instinct, the Focus, and so on—Samsung now calls every Android smartphone and tablet a Galaxy. There's the Galaxy S4 smartphone, the Galaxy

Note, the Galaxy Tab in different sizes. This brand birth control has contributed significantly to Samsung's meteoric rise in the smartphone business because the Galaxy brand has powerful equity, enough to take on the mighty iPhone. Meanwhile, rivals such as LG, HTC, and BlackBerry wallow in a sea of little-known brands. The lesson: To build a successful brand takes investment and time, so it pays to focus on a few and to invest in them over a long period.

THE FIVE FINGER RULE

Early in his career, Sanjay got a vivid lesson in the advantages of narrowing his focus. He had graduated from India's most prestigious university with plans to go to the United States to continue his studies, but to stay close to his ailing mother, he took a job in India with Unilever. The Anglo-Dutch giant started him at the bottom as a salesman and sent him to Jammu, a region in India's far north, where his assignment was to peddle soaps and detergents on a handcart to mom-and-pop stores. The routine was humbling. He'd slog from one shop to another, then stand around, hoping to place products, while the proprietor waited on customers.

Sanjay was eager to make a name, though, so for his first review, he diligently prepared a fat file of material—facts, figures, sales, and so on—and presented it to his boss, a legendary Indian sales manager who went by the initials G.P.

The boss pushed Sanjay's file aside dismissively. "How many fingers do you have on your hand?" he asked.

Dumbfounded, Sanjay asked what he meant.

"How many fingers on your hand?" G.P. repeated.

Sanjay shrugged. "Five."

"Here's the point: We will decide five things we want you to do. That's all we will measure. And I want you to put the results on one page. Five things, that's it. I don't want to see any of your details."

Sanjay realized immediately that by concentrating on the five, he was going to have to stop doing a lot of the things he'd been doing. It focused his attention, and by targeting only those five things, he had a strict, simple way to track his progress. His life quickly changed.

For more than half a century, psychologists have been arguing over whether there is something "magic" about the number seven, plus or minus two, in terms of man's ability to process information in the short term. The argument went on completely without Sanjay's knowledge. But G.P.'s lesson stayed with him: Whether you are talking about goals, directions, rules, metrics—virtually any human endeavor—keep the number small.

The argument for focus is also calling into question the strategic logic of the unfocused conglomerate. While there are still successful conglomerates like the Virgin Group, General Electric, and India's Reliance Group, these conglomerates are actually quite focused. According to Ian Rowden, the former chief marketing officer for the Virgin Group, the brand is the single asset that unifies the Virgin Group. While the hundreds of companies within it span a breathtaking array of industries and markets, the partners at the holding company ensure that the businesses conform to the unique values of the Virgin brand. Similarly, Reliance Group operates in diverse industries including petrochemicals, retail, and telecommunications. But two common themes cross all its businesses: the need for massive infrastructure, and the ability to manage large complex projects. On the other hand, more traditional diversified companies, such as ITT, Fortune Brands, Sara Lee, Tyco, Motorola, Abbott, and Kraft, are breaking up into smaller, more focused companies.

Consider Motorola. Until a few years ago, company executives insisted that their end-to-end strategy of offering handsets, infrastructure, software, and services all under one roof made sense—they could be a one-stop shop for wireless service providers such as AT&T or Vodafone. However, the infrastructure business differs fundamentally from the handset business. At its core, infrastructure is an engineering business that lives in the B2B world, with few customers, all very large. Selling is done through a direct sales force and sales cycles are years long. Customer support is on-site and customer relationships run deep. The buyers of infrastructure are executives responsible for network operations. Handsets, on the other hand, play in a fashion business, with fickle customer preferences that require rapid new product introductions and short product life cycles. Handsets are sold retail through stores, online and off, and customers number in the millions. Handset marketing looks like consumer marketing and bears little resemblance to the marketing of infrastructure. Keeping the two businesses—infrastructure and handsets—under the same roof makes little strategic sense. Motorola brought in a new CEO, Sanjay Jha, who proceeded to split Motorola up into a consumer business and an infrastructure business to sharpen its focus.

The same story is playing out in other companies. Kraft's global snacks business is growing fast, but needs investment and fast-paced innovation. The North American groceries business is a relatively slow-growth enterprise that throws off a lot of cash and needs to be managed with a close eye on costs. These businesses march to the tune of different drummers. That's why Kraft recently decided to split up into two companies that can chart different courses (Kraft for groceries with a North American base and Mondelēz International for snacks).

There's nothing magic about invoking focus. Everyone believes in it. You won't find a celebrated business guru going around shilling the advantages of muddle, disorder, and sprawl. The importance of focus gets reiterated constantly—and not just in the world of business. Basketball coaches drill their teams on the need to stay focused. Critics chide presidents for losing focus. Individuals recognize the need on their own. "Unfortunately, I lost focus about three-quarters or halfway down the course," said the brilliant American skier Lindsey Vonn after dropping out of a world championship race a few years ago.

So what is the problem?

The fact is, for companies (as for world-class athletes), staying focused can be a challenge. Often it takes courage—you have to contradict orthodoxies and fight through conventional wisdom. In its early days, Emirates met widespread industry skepticism for its premium strategy. "It's just a question of how innovative you are, how brave you are," says president Tim Clark.

Spirit Airlines looked at the low-cost leaders, Southwest and JetBlue, and asked, Why go halfway? With a relentless emphasis on passenger fees, Spirit's break-even fare by 2012 was 58 percent lower than Southwest's and 116 percent lower than JetBlue's. And though growth through consolidation has swept the airline industry, Ben Baldanza says Spirit won't be a player in that game. "Anyone who bought us would screw up our costs," he told *Flightglobal*.

Focus takes a ton of discipline. The business world is full of distractions and temptations posing as opportunities. "People get distracted by success," says Carlos Abrams-Rivera, who worked with Sanjay at Kraft. "It's human nature for people to get excited by what's new and different and chase shiny, bright objects."

At the other end of the spectrum, when trouble shows up, the urge rises to do something, anything, and if that doesn't work, try something else. Just look at the turmoil Hewlett-Packard has faced recently—four CEOs in less than a decade, lurches from one strategic initiative to another, a huge drop in market capitalization. The culprit: an acquisition binge that included buying up massive and troubled businesses, such as EDS and the dying smartphone software from Palm. The binge pushed HP into a mind-boggling array of ventures, and, as a result, HP took its eye off the ball in its core printing and personal computer businesses. Instead of the HP of old that was known for its reliable and innovative computers, servers, and printers, HP is now dabbling in everything from smartphones and tablets to outsourcing services and networking equipment. The company has lost its focus and lost its way.

HP could learn a trick or two from Xerox, the iconic inventor of copiers and photocopying, which easily could have gone the way of Kodak or Polaroid. As digital commerce and digital media threatened its core business of photocopiers and printing, Xerox could have become extinct or it could have sought out growth in unrelated businesses and stumbled. Instead, Xerox embarked on an ambitious initiative to transform itself into a business services company that allowed it to retain its traditional focus of being the "document company," while moving into the lucrative market for managing document-centric business services. Xerox now processes Medicaid insurance claims, automated toll payments, and parking tickets.

With its 2010 acquisition of Affiliated Computer Services, Xerox generates more than half its revenues by managing back-office processes and operating infrastructure on behalf of its business clients. The company handles more than 1.6 million customer interactions daily in thirty languages in 160 global customer care centers. It provides human resources services to 11 million employees and retirees. It processes 3 million credit card applications a month, 900 million health care claims each year, and 37 billion transport fares annually on buses, tramways, and subways in four hundred cities worldwide.

Although Xerox has moved aggressively into business services, it has maintained a clear and logical connection to its legacy of creating and reproducing. Seventy-five years ago, Xerox created a revolutionary way to simplify information sharing.

Today, it is focused on simplifying complex information-based business processes for its business clients. This is change with continuity, powered by focus.

Once you understand the power of focus, the question arises: Where do we begin? How should your company find the promised land? This is the journey we will undertake in this book by going through the steps of the Focus7 approach. The journey begins with the search for insights that can lead to breakthrough business opportunities.

CHAPTER 3

DISCOVERY:
SEARCH FOR GROWTH

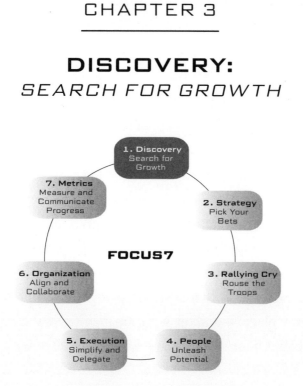

Photographers know that the best way to compose a good out-door shot is to start with a wide-angle view of the landscape and then gradually zoom in to focus on the detail that will make the most interesting subject. So it is with the journey to focus your company. The first step involves looking broadly at the landscape of opportunities to identify the most promising ones. This is the process of discovery. That leads directly to the adage we follow: Find it. Bottle it. Scale it. Search for opportunities inside the company and outside in the market-place. Identify those that seem the most promising. Then get everyone aligned behind these opportunities to scale them across the company.

INSIGHT CHANNELS

Discovery begins with insights into customers and markets that can be converted into opportunities for growth. Insights can be powerful engines for success. Multibillion-dollar companies have been founded on a single key observation. Home Depot latched onto the insight that a growing number of consumers wanted to take charge of their home improvement projects—the do-it-yourself segment that the company reached with the tagline, "You can do it. We can help." Starbucks was founded on the idea that customers would pay a premium for the "third place"—a shop with an inviting ambiance where people could hang out and enjoy a cup of coffee with friends. Netflix created a very successful DVD rental business by feeling the pain of Blockbuster customers who had been nickel-and-dimed to death with late fees on DVD rentals. Airbnb has created a thriving venture based on the insight that the underutilized space in a home could be turned into a short-term rental. As Victor Hugo famously said, "Nothing is more powerful than an idea whose time has come."

Insights can also help to scale up a company in its growth journey. Unilever's Lipton Tea division discovered that tea sales were strikingly robust in Portugal and Saudi Arabia, where, among other things, the tea was competing in the broader market of beverages, not just against rival teas. Scaling that insight in other countries led to a surge in Lipton growth. The pharmaceutical company Gilead Sciences looked at the AIDS medication business through the eyes of patients and physicians and discovered that patients had to take a cocktail of up to seventeen drugs in different daily doses that required exact sequencing. This complex drug regimen resulted in poor outcomes, even though the drugs were effective. The insight led Gilead to introduce Atripla, the first single daily dose HIV drug, an advance that has vastly improved compliance and patient quality of life. Atripla is the top HIV prescribed regimen, racking up $3.57 billion in sales in 2012 and fending off competitors from larger companies.

INSIGHT CHANNELS:
LOOKING FOR OPPORTUNITIES

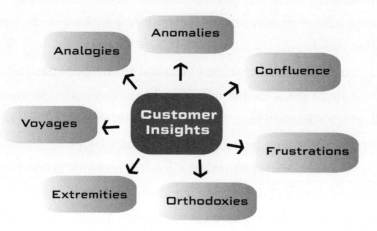

Insights often seem obvious in hindsight, but they can be hard to spot—sometimes, they are even hiding in plain sight. The trick is to see what everybody sees, but to think what nobody has thought. To set the discovery process in motion, you need insights that have the power to transform. Clearly, serendipity and intuition play an important role in spotting potential successes. But insights are too important to be left to chance. There is a method to the madness—a systematic set of analytical channels to be examined. In our collective experience, we have identified several *insight channels* that can direct and power the discovery process:

Anomalies—Virtually every company is a laboratory, a natural center of research as people try out different ideas—new products, variations in price and design, distribution changes, and so on. These experiments are often conducted in response to a problem or opportunity in a specific business unit or in a particular geographical market. Often, these natural experiments produce results that deviate significantly from business as usual. These are anomalies—variations in performance that seem odd, even surprising. They can be pregnant with opportunities.

Consider the story Mohan learned from his work with DuPont in Brazil. DuPont recognized that daily life for average Brazilians had an unfortunate anomalous element—violence is a constant threat, especially in São Paulo. People feel particularly vulnerable when driving late at night in crime-ridden neighborhoods. DuPont leveraged this insight to create an affordable way for middle-class consumers to add armor to their cars. DuPont Armura uses Kevlar to create bullet-resistant panels that are light, flexible, and molded for a precise fit. The DuPont Armura car armor kit helps provide protection against gunshots from 97 percent of all firearms used in violent crimes. The entire package weighs less than two hundred pounds and costs $12,000, far cheaper and lighter than traditional armor. What's more, the dealer can install the armor kit quickly after the car has been bought. Armura responds to an anomalous situation with an anomalous product—something that doesn't exist in other markets, but makes perfect sense in crime-ridden São Paulo.

In other cases, you may have to look outside your company for productive anomalies. The key is to pore over market data. Where are the numbers out of whack? What's surprising? Is the market penetration of a product oddly high or low? Is a particular customer segment flocking to or balking at a new product? Are men and women responding differently to a product? Then dig. Try to figure out the basis for the unusual results.

Whirlpool learned this when it was exploring opportunities for growth. The company discovered that while people worry about the impression made by the appearance of their home, the concern doesn't extend to their garages. The justification: The mess in the garage is what allows their homes to look neat and organized! Besides, what else could you do with a garage? This anomaly led Whirlpool to explore how to extend that sense of fastidiousness from the home to the garage. How could the garage become valuable extra space that could increase the resale value of the house? Whirlpool's answer lay in a new business called Gladiator GarageWorks that offers a range of storage and organization products to transform garages into lifestyle spaces for the auto enthusiast, the sports fanatic, or the gardener with the green thumb. Gladiator GarageWorks has emerged as one of Whirlpool's most successful new businesses of recent years. It all started with an anomaly—why is it acceptable to have a neat house with a messy garage? Consumers accepted this as a fact of life, because they could not imagine that they could have a neat house *and* an organized garage!

Confluence—When surging trends come together—or can be put together—the intersection can produce an opportunity. Consider, for example, the three most significant trends in digital content and services today—the *social, local,* and *mobile sectors,* often referred to as SoLoMo. The intersection has spawned dozens of valued start-up businesses. A few examples: Social meets mobile to create Groupon, the discount site. Social meets mobile video to create Snapchat and Vine, services that allow short videos to be exchanged socially. Mobile meets local to create Foursquare, a service that helps you save the places you visit and share them with your friends. And so on. If you can find two or more trends that are coming together, you can be quite sure that the intersection can be mined for valuable insights.

Frustrations—Points of pain or inconvenience are fruitful sources of opportunities. Look for areas where potential customers don't have a good way to solve a problem. Mark Vadon, the founder of Blue Nile, the online diamond and jewelry company, was one of those customers. In the late nineties, he went shopping for an engagement ring, but found the in-store experience off-putting. It turns out many men shared his frustration. Understanding how diamonds are categorized and valued is a complicated business; plus, the little rocks are expensive. For a purchaser—often a man who goes into the process blind—there is much to learn, and getting pressured by a store salesperson only aggravates the experience. Vadon turned his frustration into BlueNile.com, which offers custom-ers reams of information about diamonds and tens of thou-sands of choices at relatively lower cost, with absolutely no sales pressure. Today, Blue Nile is the largest online retailer of diamonds.

Frustration-based businesses abound. Netflix, the video rental and streaming service, was created because Reed Hast-ings, its cofounder, was annoyed with the late fees that Block-buster slapped on him for DVD rentals. Salesforce.com, one of the fastest-growing software companies in history, capitalized on the frustration that companies felt with the available soft-ware for managing customer relationships, which cost millions of dollars, took years to install, and remained painful to main-tain. Salesforce.com created a new service that eliminated the need to buy, install, and maintain expensive software because the software was delivered over a network and paid for by a monthly subscription. The company has continued to grow by addressing related frustrations with software for marketing, customer service, and social networking within a company.

Orthodoxies—Sometimes taking a piece of common wisdom

or practice and turning it on its head can open surprising doors. You may find that something no longer makes sense in a changing world. Or your contrarianism may lead the way to a new market. Capella Hotels and Resorts, which operates small, luxury facilities in prime spots around the world, wondered why hotels and motels traditionally have a regular check-in time—anywhere from noon to four P.M. After all, guests don't always arrive or leave on a set schedule that accommodates the hospitality routine. The orthodoxy grew out of the fact that if guests checked in when they wanted, the cleaning staff would be banging around at all hours, hence disturbing guests who were already settled. So Capella came up with a simple but profound solution: Soundproof every room. Operate housekeeping and laundry around the clock. The result: Check-in is at the convenience of the guest—an innovation that differentiates Capella from its competition for business travelers.

Law firms are the paragon of orthodoxies. They operate as partnerships, hire associates fresh out of law school, put them on the partner track, and measure performance in terms of billable hours per year. A new age law firm called Axiom is discovering opportunities by turning these orthodoxies on their head. Axiom formed as a kind of white-shoe temp agency, offering up its associated lawyers for top-tier projects that could be short-term or even take months. The lawyers work from home or in the offices of the client, bringing down Axiom's overhead (and hence its fees). Clients like the fact that Axiom doesn't come with the overhead of Big Law and that the work is done by specialized and experienced lawyers. Lawyers like working for Axiom because they can pick and choose their work, their clients, and their schedules without worrying about the constant need to drum up business and rack up billable hours. Axiom lawyers—now numbering around six hundred—come from the best law schools and some of the major firms, and many clients are Fortune 500 companies.

Extremities—Most companies spend too much time with their mainstream customers and not enough time studying the folks on the fringes. The fact is, there are customers you earn from and customers you learn from. The customers you learn from are often at the fringes of your customer base. They are the weird people who are either extreme users of your products or the folks who rarely if ever buy anything from you or even from your competitors.

At the high end, these customers can be demanding, but often they are ahead of the curve, showing you where you should go. Over the years, for example, the auto manufacturers have stayed close to the world of racing, using it to get ideas and test them on the track, everything from auto safety features to innovations in engine technology. Similarly, a slew of technology start-ups have been created in the security software business with Israel Defense Force to thank.

At the low end, the infrequent customer can teach ways to broaden the market. For example, Nokia's effort to introduce phones to villages in India has led to several innovations. Much of rural India lacks street lighting, so Nokia came up with the idea to equip phones with flashlights to help people get around at night. The company also began producing phones that had radio reception—home entertainment. Recently, Nokia in India has been introducing phones that allow transfers of money from one phone to another—making the phone an increasingly valuable tool in areas where banks are few and far between.

Voyages—There's much to be learned if you get out of the building and immerse yourself in the day-to-day life of your customers. After all, Columbus had to get on a ship and sail across the ocean to discover America. To understand people, you need to see them in a land that can be unfamiliar to a company—where they live and where they work. What you find will often take you well beyond surveys and focus groups.

A classic example for this category comes from Xerox, which was an early pioneer in hiring ethnographers to better track the way people actually use technology. In the 1980s, as Xerox searched for breakthrough ideas, it sent out teams of ethnographers to study the way people worked with printers. The studies were done in client offices—natural surroundings, so to speak. The researchers found that when printers jammed, many people were baffled about how to fix them—the process seemed intimidating, though in fact it was not difficult. The solution: Create a common design language to make the copiers easier to use and operate. Xerox photocopiers now feature doors with obvious handles. Color coding distinguishes different areas of the copier: Areas for original documents are green, areas where paper is loaded are blue, and areas for the copy output are red. The improvement in usability was dramatic—paper jams that took twenty-eight minutes to fix before the redesign took a mere twenty seconds afterward. The by-product of this usability improvement—users were more tolerant of paper jams when they did occur, because it was so easy to fix them!

Analogies—Look around at other industries. Is there something that works in another line of business that might translate neatly into yours? Sometimes you find practices that are par for the course in one field, but that nobody has thought to introduce to your market.

Cemex, a cement company based in Mexico, found inspiration from well outside its industry as it struggled with a vexing problem in the ready-mix concrete business. Because construction is an erratic and unreliable business—among other things, the weather disruptions—customers would cancel or reschedule almost half their Cemex orders at the last minute. What could Cemex do with a truckful of liquid concrete that the customer no longer needed? After all, liquid concrete can't just go back on the shelf.

Cemex looked at other industries that are good at quick response. Their inspiration came from Houston's emergency response center, where dispatchers could send a team of paramedics to the site of an accident within ten minutes with high reliability. What made this possible was a dispatch network. Cemex seized upon this insight and installed GPS locator devices in its trucks, connecting them to the company's command center through a satellite-based tracking system. Now, Cemex can see its fleet in real time and dispatch a truck to an order when and as needed. If the order is canceled, the truck simply gets rerouted in transit to the closest customer. The analogy: Dispatch cement trucks in the same way emergency responders dispatch crews or taxi fleet operators dispatch taxis. There's a lot you can learn by applying ideas from strange and faraway industries to your business.

DISCOVERY IN ACTION AT HYATT HOTELS

The search for promising innovations should be going on all the time in any business. Discovery should be a constant. To press that process, we recommend distributing the list of insight channels to employees, perhaps using examples drawn from your own business. You may even recognize some channels that we have overlooked. Hold an occasional meeting aimed at emphasizing the importance of innovation discovery. Good ideas can come from anyone and from anywhere, so you want people in your company to have their antennae up always. Having the list of insight channels in front of everyone helps keep the search top of mind.

Often during a time of transition, a company will go through a systematic discovery process. That was the case recently with the Hyatt Hotels Corporation. After Hyatt went public in 2009, the CEO, Mark S. Hoplamazian, set as a goal for the company to earn the customer ranking of "most preferred" in all the categories in which it competes. To get a reckoning of where Hyatt stood, the company commissioned a brand health study that surveyed a large sample of hotel customers to understand how Hyatt was perceived relative to its key competitors in the hotel industry. The results were disturbing: Hyatt, like the hospitality business in general, was adrift in a sea of sameness. "It had become a highly commoditized industry," says Jeff Semenchuk, who joined Hyatt as chief innovation officer in 2011. Research showed that "hotels are run very mechanically, very much by scripts and operating procedures, and in fact not much had changed within the last twenty to thirty years."

So Hyatt set in motion an intense discovery process to find where the opportunities lay. The process started with interviews of guests who ran the gamut, from the business traveler to family vacationers. The news was often painful. In terms of the insight channels highlighted above, the potential opportunities poured forth in customer *frustrations*. One of the most piercing messages came back from women: You don't get us. Hotels are designed by men for men. Women's concerns remain an afterthought, even though women have increasingly joined the ranks of business travelers. The toiletries are inadequate. The robes don't fit. Room service deliveries are usually by men, raising privacy issues. The list went on.

Other guest frustrations applied to both sexes. Checking into a hotel interrupted the digital lives of guests. Many of the older, big, full-service hotels were built before the Internet and Wi-Fi. Guests arrived and their connections stopped or cost too much to keep up. On another front, the guests' wellness routines were disrupted—they couldn't get their healthy breakfasts or arrange for their usual course of exercise. "What a horrible thing to say—we sent you home in worse shape than when you arrived!" Semenchuk says. Even the format of business meetings—a key source of revenue at some Hyatt Hotels—drew complaints. The technology didn't work. The room setup was awkward. The meeting experience in general seemed outdated. "You squint and you could still be having a meeting in the eighties," says Semenchuk.

Hyatt also tapped into the guest experience from the other direction, seeking insights from colleagues on the front lines every day. In more than forty sessions around the globe, Hyatt brought together groups of five to ten Hyatt employees with a diversity of levels, roles, ages, and experience. Each session focused on a theme—the digital experience, for example—and the participants were set loose to generate ideas. "We'd do a very quick tutorial to say a concept or an idea isn't just a bunch of bullet points on a flip chart," Semenchuk recalls. "It's a well-formed concept that includes: Who is it for? What is the need that it's addressing? What are the features of this concept? What are the six or seven most important things?"

Semenchuk and his colleagues who organized the sessions came up with a little test: When participants in the sessions suggested an idea, they were asked to give it a name and sketch it on a piece of paper—a single sheet. "We said that if someone who wasn't part of the session came up and looked at it, the sheet of paper should be sufficient for them to say, 'Oh, I get it.'"

By the end of the discovery process, Hyatt had collected dozens of ideas and insights, from big to small. Ideas included ways to choose and check into rooms, to use digital technology to enhance the guest experience, to improve staffing, and to improve the quality of room service. Some ideas were duplicative. Many were incremental. Some would have been downright disruptive. But now the company was equipped with potential opportunities that could be clustered or winnowed down to a manageable number, as we will discuss in the next chapter.

FROM INSIGHTS TO ACTION— DISCOVERY WORKSHOPS

We've pointed out several routes to structuring your search for productive insights. But insights only start the discovery process. To turn insights into action, you need to align people behind specific opportunities. Alignment is the side to discovery that is often overlooked and equally important. The greatest innovation, the freshest idea, likely falters if the company managers don't see the direction and push for it.

Almost a decade before Apple launched the iPhone, development teams within Nokia had foreseen the future of smartphones. They had developed a phone with a color touch screen set above a single button. The device could be used to find restaurants, play games, and shop online. And that wasn't the only promising product developed by Nokia. In the late 1990s, the company had come up with a tablet computer with a wireless connection and touch screen—everything that Apple put into the blockbuster iPad in 2010. But the development teams could not get the attention of the leadership to act on the insights. Intoxicated by its success in feature phones and believing that it had mastered the success formula in the phone business, Nokia's leaders failed to capitalize on the insights that pointed toward a very different future for smartphones and devices. The result—Nokia is a mere shadow of its former self and struggles to survive in a world that turned out very close to what some of its people had predicted.

Sadly, you can't eat insights for lunch. Getting from insights to market success requires leadership commitment and solid execution. Eventually, the focus will have to be transmitted throughout the organization, but it has to start with the leadership. Insights and alignment go hand in hand. Together, they constitute the work of discovery.

There are many ways to bring together insights and alignment—a remarkable leader such as Steve Jobs, for example, could do it through his own force of will. But business geniuses come along rarely. For the rest of us, it helps to have a mechanism to get the process going. Through experience, we have found that carefully managed workshops, one to two days in length, can be such a mechanism. Sometimes these workshops take place after new ideas and directions have been uncovered using the insight channels that we have discussed. Sometimes the workshops generate discoveries in their own right.

Workshops have become staples of the business world. With their numbing PowerPoint presentations, their reams of paper lists tacked to the walls, their endlessly repeated exhortations, workshops typically provoke silent groans. We are aware of that, but handled right, workshops can be extraordinarily useful in promoting innovation and moving operations forward. Their impact can have a ripple effect, as the participants take a hand in devising the new direction and pass on that sense of ownership throughout the company. In short, workshops rank as a prime tool in kicking off the drive for focus. "The discovery workshop can be extraordinarily effective, not just in getting the process going, but in setting the direction and tone of the whole transformation," says Pradeep Pant, a veteran of the workshop experience who was president of Kraft Asia Pacific.

Over three decades at Unilever, Fonterra Brands, and Kraft, Sanjay refined the workshop process and used it with consistent success. A prime example came when he joined Kraft and took charge of the floundering international markets business in 2007. He started by making the traditional corporate tour of the properties, visiting Kraft's key outposts around the world. At each stop, he asked regional executives to name their priority initiatives. He drew on the Five Finger Rule he'd learned starting out—he asked the executives to name just three to five priorities, a list that could be counted on one hand. Even limited like that, everyone's list was different. The exercise serves as a simple but powerful test to see if your company is aligned. And Kraft was badly out of alignment.

Though the company featured a roster of skilled employees and a valued collection of brands, Kraft had grown so big and scattered that promising ideas disappeared or got watered down. At a time when the company was moving aggressively onto the global stage, too many decisions came out of headquarters in Northfield, Illinois, in suburban Chicago. The voices of consumers in, say, Germany or China weren't being heard. Overall, too many wheels were spinning without enough forward motion.

To get things moving, Sanjay brought together Kraft's regional leaders for workshops at six locations around the world. He bolstered each gathering with the input of vendors, consultants, investment bankers, and consumers. The workshops featured no preconceived notions by Sanjay or other Kraft executives. The goal was simple: to discover likely opportunities toward which to channel resources, and, conversely, to isolate aspects of the business that weren't working. The workshops "are not preorganized around an outcome that you are trying to sell to people," says George Zoghbi, who has participated in workshops at both Fonterra and Kraft and is now president of Kraft's North American cheese division. "They are a forum to organize ideas and whittle them down to areas of focus."

Those workshops became the petri dish that generated the 5-10-10 strategy for Kraft Developing Markets—the plan to focus on five categories, ten brands, and ten markets. Similarly, Fonterra used workshops to hone its plan to focus on 5 power brands among the 150 brands in its portfolio.

We should point out that the workshop process can serve powerfully for smaller units, too—not just the entire company. The approach can be applied to functions within a company— say, a production department that is having problems meeting deadlines. The level or size of the department makes no difference. Similarly, the process can be particularly useful to a start-up, since many start-ups—regardless of industry—have trouble settling on their core business.

But workshops don't run themselves. They can easily fall into the tedium and time wasting that provoke those silent groans mentioned earlier. Or they can turn into gripe sessions or toxic outbreaks of blame. The tone must remain positive throughout.

To stay on track, an effective workshop needs to be carefully choreographed. To do that, we have developed a number of techniques and principles. Some of these may sound familiar or obvious, but in practice many are overlooked. Here they are:

Set clear goals—This is important, but easily missed. The goal, or purpose, of the workshop should be clear and laid out for all participants. As we'll see, getting there will mean navigating a sea of turmoil, but the destination should always be visible. The goal should neither be too broad and generic (e.g., "How can we be more innovative?" or "How do we improve profit margins?") nor too tactical (e.g., "How can we drive adoption of a new product?" or "How do we grow our business in Argentina?"). Some of the best goals concentrate on spreading success. "How do we duplicate the efficiencies established at our Potterville factory?" And a goal aimed at focus usually works well. "Which three products under our Widget brand have the most potential for growth?"

Right people—The relevant leaders of the unit involved should participate, but it's also important to include some up-and-comers, people who are less accustomed to the company's traditional ways of thinking. Along those same lines, bring in a few iconoclasts to help animate discussions and generate fresh ideas. Diversity of opinion sparks thinking—to get new conversations going, introduce new people. Overall, you want to bring together smart and capable people, some of whom wouldn't otherwise get the chance to sit down together and share ideas.

Right size—We've found that workshops function best with an agile facilitator and no more than twenty people—enough to get a range of voices, but not so many that some don't get heard.

Right length—Though a well-organized workshop offers plenty to digest and discuss and could easily run for several days, we find that keeping the time frame short adds a useful sense of urgency. Participants need to get comfortable with cutting to the chase, getting to the heart of the matter. We recommend holding the workshop to one day or perhaps two if the issues to be discussed are particularly complex.

Mute the boss—This marks a fundamental difference from conventional workshops, but it's essential. While all participants should engage in the discussion, the boss should remain muted and in the background. The point is to let the discussion roam without regard to past practices or current favorite initiatives. Even the body language of the ranking executive can tilt the proceedings and inhibit the openness that's necessary for best results. Still, the boss has an important role and should be there. He listens and learns. He provides clarification where necessary. If something goes off agenda, he can help keep it on track.

Spread the net wide in gathering data—Well ahead of time, the organizers should gather a range of potentially useful data and reports related to the state of the business and the objectives of the workshop. These might include financial records; reports on products, brands, markets, operations; customer and vendor surveys; analysts' reports; news accounts. Benchmarks, both internal and external, are crucial. Be creative. Often headquarters gets fixated on the usual metrics or the traditional measures. This is the time to break away from that—to change the frame of reference. If material has been gathered through other insight channels—voyages, antiorthodoxies, etc.—it should be included here.

Do the homework—This vital rule too often gets disregarded in the hurly-burly. The background material—the homework—should be distributed to workshop participants ahead of time, along with a brief outline of the workshop's objectives. And the organizers must make it absolutely clear: Participants are expected to read the material beforehand. They must arrive prepared. The workshop hours are then devoted to tapping the knowledge and intelligence of the people in the room, not to the sharing of facts, which would be a ludicrous waste of time when everyone is perfectly capable of examining the data on his or her own.

We can't overemphasize the necessary role played by the homework. "It's important to put everyone on an equal footing," says George Zoghbi. "It's important they understand that these are all hard facts—this is what the reality is. Now, come, let's talk about it."

With proper preparation, the answers to most of the questions that come up—and ideas for moving forward—can almost always be found in the data or teased out of the background material.

Mining for gold—Virtually all companies, even ones that are underperforming, have islands of excellence that can become the basis of sustained growth. The discovery workshop offers the chance to explore for successes, particularly those that may have been overlooked. We call this "mining for gold." The prospecting usually starts with the data homework: What stands out? What's unusual? What's beating benchmarks? What's surprising? The point is to find potential opportunities and then try to build them and replicate them elsewhere.

We have a phrase to describe this course of action, and we will repeat it more than once in these pages: Find it. Bottle it. Scale it.

Chaos is your friend—This can be a hard point to grasp, and the experience can easily flummox managers used to disciplined, rational, even programmed discussions. In the early hours of the workshop, the ideas, thoughts, and conversations should be wide-ranging and open-ended. Free associative. Messy. Illogical. "The best way I can describe it is organized chaos with a purpose," says Carlos Abrams-Rivera, who went through the workshop experience at Kraft. The point is to make people uncomfortable enough to move beyond their usual responses, to come up with ideas that weren't in their heads when they walked into the workshop. "We're pushing people to think differently, telling them, 'Hey, if you're going to make a statement, tell me more about it. No, we don't need opinions. We need you to back it up with why you think that way.'"

The facilitator should be armed with questions designed to provoke fresh discussion. Occasionally, the facilitator and the leaders will need to confer during breaks to assess whether the chaos has prompted the necessary fresh thinking. If the momentum slows, the leaders need to come up with other provocative questions to churn things up again.

One technique that can be effective is to ask participants to imagine the future. For example, ask the manager of a regional business to assume it's three years from this day and the numbers are terrific. How did she do it? Typically, someone pressed in this way will respond in generalities—improved cash flow, more efficient production, et cetera. Press for specifics and keep pressing. The ideas usually start to flow.

No holds barred—Participants should know that they are welcome to bring up subjects that can be controversial or painful. Lorna Davis points out that at Kraft historically there was a "low level of maturity around honest and open conversation. There is an avoidance of conflict and there is a desire to be rational or to portray things as rational when we all know that life isn't very rational." The workshop gave participants the opportunity "to discuss the undiscussable," as she puts it.

The conversation has to move beyond platitudes. If a competitor is doing better in some aspect of the business, ask why. The idea isn't to inject conflict, but to encourage thinking and discussion about the hard facts. If the business lags the marketplace, ask what three things could be done to catch up.

Make clear from the start that the workshops are blame-free zones. No one is there to point fingers. Knowledgeable people have gathered together to chew over issues and look for answers. The workshop operates on the assumption that everyone is the solution, not the problem—make sure that message gets repeated.

Sharpening the thinking—After a few hours of free-flowing ideas, the facilitator should start to narrow the discussion. At this point, there are several questions to use as tools to sharpen the thinking.

Why? When people have identified successes, ask them to explain why. Employees are always quick to suggest that their victories are the exception to the rule, not something the rest of the company can learn from. They're wrong. Press them.

What are the similarities? Push the participants to look for parallels among the ideas and success stories. Try to connect dots. Identify patterns. The point is to find hidden strengths that can be extracted and used elsewhere.

Another key exercise: Ask participants to imagine ways to test their theories. Are there actual experiments that could be run? (There's that business-as-lab concept again.) This type of thinking may be new to many employees, and the discussion may again seem scattered and fruitless. Keep going. The exercise hones analytical skills that will redound to the long-term advantage of the company.

What's not working—Though the emphasis of the workshop should be determinedly positive, you need to isolate what's not working, too. In any company, initiatives stall, brands decline, processes ossify. Sometimes companies end up with unproductive practices that just seem to develop over time without much thought attached. Examining the failures and roadblocks—without casting blame or slipping into a gripe session—serves as a key driver of focus.

Don't let this drag out. We recommend devoting no more than about 30 percent of the workshop time to what's not working. The process should follow the same methodology—ask why the problem has developed and push the room to look for solutions. The workshop participants should be able to draw on one another's experiences. At one Kraft workshop, for example, participants spent time considering shortcomings in Kraft Germany. It became clear that local management had grown too internally focused, worried about what headquarters would think, not looking out the window at the actual customer. With advice from Kraft leaders in other markets, the German managers were able to right the course.

Stick to the schedule—This can be tough to enforce, as discussions could easily drag on beyond the allotted time, but it's important. Holding to the timetable imparts discipline and focus. When an issue comes up that's not readily resolved, the participants should decide whether to:

- sort it out now with as much specificity as possible;
- plan to get a plan of action to deal with it; or
- park it—put it aside and leave it for another time.

Above all, don't use the meeting to argue over things that can't be helped. Remember the Hindi admonition: *Karna Kya Hai?*—"*So what do we do now?*"

Summing up—The last hour or so of the workshop should be devoted to summing up: What did we achieve today? What are the strategic initiatives that we've isolated? What are the next steps? When are we going to take them? A careful balance needs to be struck between "let's get on with it urgently," which can result in emphasizing tactics over strategy, and "let's plan to discuss," which can leave too much ambiguity and too many loose ends.

Everyone should walk out of the room with agreement on the fundamentals, and the summary should be exactly that—a summary, an elevator speech, to use the popular term. And even the elevator speech needs to hold to G.P.'s Five Finger Rule.

The summary nails down the necessary alignment—it assures that, after a day or so of discussion, the participants agree with what has unfolded. And the summary sets the table for what is to ensue. "By the time they leave the workshop, everybody should be reading from the same playbook," says Gustavo Abelenda, president of Kraft Latin America.

Kraft's 2007 workshops produced a clear plan with various teams and leaders given clear responsibilities, action items, and time frames. Here's the basic elevator speech delivered at the conclusion: "We are trying to do too many things. We want to try to focus on a limited number of categories, brands, and markets which in the next three to five years will contribute a significant part of our sales and profits. We need to align resources—money, talent, and expertise—against those key priorities. We have identified a short list of priorities that we will refine in the next four weeks. We will align resources—money, talent, and expertise—against those key priorities and create a plan to manage the others."

If that message sounds totally simple and straightforward—well, that's the point at this stage. Specific areas of focus, as well as strategies and action plans, will come later, after more discussion, as described in the next step in the following chapter. It's smart not to rush into specific actions too quickly, as that may only result in a series of short-term tactical actions. What's important now is that all participants are on board about the process and feel party to the search for solutions. Whatever eventual priorities are established, they'll only be effective if there's a shared sense of ownership and cocreation. Later, a smaller team will refine priorities, capture the nuggets from the workshops, and start working with the larger group to develop a road map for implementation.

Family—We know it sounds schmaltzy, but we talk about building a sense of family—the feeling that everyone has a role, everyone has responsibilities, and we're all in this together. That elusive cohesion should grow and spread from the workshop participants and eventually help align the entire business.

We recommend holding a dinner for participants the evening the workshop concludes. The agenda remains loose—let the day's conversations continue as people build on the ideas on the table. Maybe a few new ones will come up. But this isn't a social gathering. Staying with the relentless emphasis on the positive, it's an opportunity for leaders to single out people who have managed masterfully or units that have outperformed benchmarks. The most powerful motivator is so-called positive shame—the very human drive to earn recognition to rival the acclaim lavished on the other guy. That combination of peer pressure and togetherness requires a somewhat delicate balance, but the two forces are behind most winning companies.

The journey of discovery needs insights to get started, but the workshops put ideas into action. By combining a rich process of generating insights with a disciplined process of examining ideas through discovery workshops, you are well on your way to finding transformational growth opportunities.

The next step is to synthesize the insights and potential opportunities that came up in the workshop, combining and narrowing the ideas until they form a well-wrought strategy.

STEP 1—DISCOVERY:
SEARCH FOR GROWTH

1. The search for growth begins with customer and market insights that can be converted into growth opportunities.
2. Insights can be serendipitous, but you can't leave them to chance. You can improve the odds of gaining insights by methodically exploring a range of key sources.
3. Key sources of insight include: anomalies, confluence, frustrations, orthodoxies, extremities, voyages, and analogies.

4. To convert insights into opportunities, bring people together in a discovery workshop to identify the opportunities contained in the insights and to create a shared understanding of the opportunity.

5. Leaders play a key role as catalysts in discovery, but they need to step back and let the teams drive the discovery process.

CHAPTER 4

STRATEGY:
PICK YOUR BETS

In the early 2000s, Michael Dell invited Mohan to speak to Dell's leadership team about marketing strategy. During the conversation with the team, Mohan remarked that Dell's R&D budget of a few hundred million dollars was a minuscule percentage of revenues, much smaller than the R&D spending of other technology companies, such as Microsoft, Hewlett-Packard, and Intel. Michael Dell offered an unexpected response. He noted that the leadership was proud that the company spent so little on R&D while generating tens of billions in revenue. Why? "We are a supply chain company first and foremost. We focus on two key capabilities—building computers to order and delivering them direct to our customers with no middlemen. We don't win by being first to the market with innovative products. We win by running the most cost-efficient supply chain and distribution channels."

To view Dell as a product innovator is the wrong way to look at the company. When you examine Dell through the lens of the supply chain and distribution channels, its strategy comes into sharp focus. This is the power of a lens—the term we use to refer to a particular dimension of the business. Lenses help companies prioritize opportunities and define the dimensions along which they focus their growth strategy.

At the conclusion of the discovery process discussed in the previous chapter, a company will end up with a broad assortment of ideas and concepts—opportunities that have the potential to be drivers of growth. The challenge now is to structure those possibilities into a manageable set of themes. Put another way: Discovery is about *divergence*—brainstorming, exploring, breaking away from orthodoxies, collecting ideas from all directions. The next step is about *convergence*—bringing promising ideas together so there are a handful of growth initiatives on which to focus. Then the heavyweights, the best ideas, can each be analyzed according to their likely business impact and the effort required in carrying them out.

We have found that the best mechanism for creating convergence is to look at the opportunity landscape through a few key lenses. The vantage point allows you to examine opportunities from various angles, isolating the assorted pros and cons and highlighting connections. Instead of a broad landscape of possibilities, you focus on a few.

Here's why this is so important: Extra resources—money, people, skills, attention—will be channeled toward those focus initiatives. We call this concept *distorting resources*. The idea is really quite simple. Remove resources from areas that are struggling or just getting by and don't hold much promise to turn around. Stop the small stuff—the hobbies that are going nowhere. Give disproportionate resources to initiatives that have the potential for profitable growth. Fuel this through continuously looking at ways to keep processes simple and costs lean. Phase execution to ensure there is a balance between investment and profit, always ensuring healthy gross margins. We'll explore the distorting-resources concept in more detail in chapter 6 and show how, in special instances, the distortion behind a select project can seem startlingly out of whack (though always with appropriate controls). But the underlying proposition is just common sense: Put your efforts where you have the best chance of winning big.

Returning to our discussion of convergence, Mohan and some of his business school colleagues have spent the past decade reflecting on how companies grow and how they innovate. This research has led to an inventory of eight key lenses through which a company can focus opportunities. These eight lenses, taken together, define the key dimensions of a business and represent a complete checklist of potential ways to focus efforts to innovate and grow.

Before we take a deep dive into the strategy lenses, let's look at the way discovery and focusing through lenses has unfolded so far at Hyatt Hotels Corporation.

In the preceding chapter, we talked about the discovery process that Hyatt went through to come up with ways to differentiate itself from competitors and grow its market share. By the end of this discovery process, Hyatt had collected an array of ideas of varying value. The challenge then was to group or select the dozens of ideas and come up with a manageable number of contenders that could each be evaluated for impact and effort. Looking through lenses became a key to that winnowing process.

To start, Hyatt relied on the *customer* lens. Specifically, several ideas in the discovery process centered on women guests traveling on business. As we discussed in the previous chapter, women had expressed a variety of frustrations with their hotel experience, ranging from privacy to safety to the quality of amenities. When Hyatt looked at the opportunities through the lens of the women business traveler segment, it found a strong theme centered on creating the "ideal hotel for women business travelers"—which provided a clear focus for further pursuit of opportunities.

Another lens that Hyatt used was the *process* of managing the customer experience at every "moment of truth"—from the point at which customers looked for a hotel to the point at which they left the hotel. For example, the discovery findings indicated that guests appreciated feeling that service was somehow personalized. That led to the notion: What would happen if the front desk agents were freed from a checklist of responses and allowed to read the emotional state of an arriving guest? Is he or she tired, frustrated, feeling chatty? The agent could then treat the guest in the manner that seemed best suited to the situation. Similarly, in a world full of smartphones and tablets, Hyatt came up with several ideas for creating a "digital guest experience" that leveraged technology to create a proactive, personalized, and pleasing guest experience. For example, why not arrange for ordering room service from a smartphone? Or allow online check-in with a smartphone application, so a guest could enter his or her room without interacting with any Hyatt employee?

The effort put in motion by Mark Hoplamazian to reinvigorate the company—to escape the sea of sameness—is still in its early stages. But already Hyatt is testing specific initiatives at a handful of so-called lab hotels around the globe. Eventually, each initiative will need to be evaluated for impact—the revenue potential—and the effort that would be required to scale the project up. "We've created filters that include asking, for instance, if we did this concept or if we had this particular focus area, how big could it be?" says Hyatt's Jeff Semenchuk. He offers an example: "If we had a choice to do something more for single women travelers versus guests regardless of gender who are coming to us to attend meetings, where would we get the biggest payback?"

THE EIGHT STRATEGY LENSES

Dell focused its business by looking at it through the lens of channels and the supply chain process. Hyatt focused its opportunity landscape by looking through the lenses of customer segments and the customer experience process. But what are all the possible lenses that each company could have considered? Is there a complete list of lenses that can be systematically assessed for clustering growth opportunities? Yes.

To understand the list of strategy lenses, let's get back to basics. What is a business? As we described in chapter 1, a business produces *something* of value *somehow* and sells it *somewhere* to *somebody*. These are the four fundamental dimensions of a business—the *What*, the *How*, the *Where*, and the *Who*. As you'll see, within each dimension we define two more specific subdimensions:

- The WHAT: These are the offerings that a company creates. Within this dimension, we define two subdimensions— the company's products and its brands. For instance, Procter & Gamble has its oral care brand Crest, which it uses for a range of products including toothpaste, toothbrushes, and whitening strips.
- The WHO: These are the audiences to which a company markets its products. This dimension includes the com-

pany's customers and its partners. Microsoft's customers include enterprises, small businesses, and consumers. Its partners include an array of system integrators, distributors, and independent software vendors.

- The WHERE: These are the geographic markets in which a company operates and the channels it uses to get to them. Microsoft, for instance, has more than one hundred geographic market subsidiaries around the world and uses a variety of channels, including original equipment manufacturers (OEMs), value-added resellers (VARs), direct sales force, retailers, and online sales.

- The HOW: These are the processes the company uses to operate and the monetization mechanisms it uses to make money. Processes cover all internal systems for managing customers, people, finances, information technology, and operations. Monetization mechanisms include product sales, advertising, subscription revenues, and newer innovations, such as the "freemium" model (offering a free version of the service, but enticing customers to upgrade to a paid version).

These eight specific dimensions are the "lenses" that a company can use to focus on growth opportunities. The four categories and the eight lenses are shown in the figure below.

Let's understand each of these lenses and see how they can be used as a tool to focus your growth and innovation strategy.

Offerings: A company produces something of value that it offers to its marketplace. This can be a product (such as a

THE EIGHT STRATEGY LENSES

WHAT
① OFFERING
② BRANDS

WHO
③ CUSTOMERS
④ PARTNERS

WHERE
⑤ CHANNELS
⑥ MARKETS

HOW
⑦ MONETIZATION
⑧ PROCESSES

refrigerator or shampoo), a service (such as logistics services or management consulting services), a platform upon which derivative products and services can be built (such as the Android platform or Amazon's Web Services platform), or a solution (such as kitchen remodeling solutions from Home Depot or safety and protection solutions from DuPont). For nonprofit or government organizations, the offering may be more abstract. The FBI's offering is "National Security." The Chicago Public Schools' offering is "Education."

Offerings are a popular lens through which to focus strategy because most large companies tend to have hundreds, even thousands, of products and services. Often, only a few offer disproportionate potential for growth and profits. If the discovery process suggests a set of offerings with which the company can win and grow, then the offering lens is a logical basis to focus strategy. For instance, the pharmacy giant Walgreens sells a broad assortment of products, from food to cosmetics to photography supplies, but most are stocked only because they attract customers looking to fill prescriptions. Prescriptions account for over 60 percent of Walgreens' sales and an even larger percentage of profits. Walgreens fills one in five prescriptions in the United States. So as it plans to win and grow, the offerings (more specifically, its prescription drug offerings) provide one lens through which Walgreens should look at its growth strategy.

Brands: Some of the most valuable assets that a company can own are its brands. Brands are intangible assets that live in the minds and hearts of its customers. And for some companies, brands can serve as powerful growth engines, accommodating line extensions and extensions beneath the brand umbrella. Consumer packaged goods companies live and die by their brands, as do service companies and many technology companies. The key here is to create *Brands with Soul*—in other words, to build on a simple consumer insight that provides an emotional connection and remains relevant for generations.

Consider a company like the Virgin Group, founded by the irrepressible Richard Branson. Virgin is a loose confederation of companies in a diverse set of industries, ranging from mobile telephones to financial services to music to space travel. The glue that holds this confederation together is the brand. Virgin stands for innovation, value, fun, and excellence in the customer experience. Seen through the offering lens, Virgin seems quite unfocused, as it is all over the place in terms of products, services, and industries. And, indeed, there may be an opportunity to focus the portfolio. But when you look at

Virgin through the brand lens, the logic becomes evident. For Virgin, the brand is the key platform for growth and innovation. This is the lens that matters.

Customers: The customers that a company serves can also provide an important lens for focusing growth efforts. Customers can be defined in terms of segments (such as baby boomers, women, or technology enthusiasts), size (small business, midmarket, and enterprise), role (IT professionals or salespeople), or behaviors and motivations (do-it-yourselfers, commuters, or risk-averse customers). Looking at your customers or their needs in an innovative way can become a powerful engine for growth.

Consider Enterprise Rent-A-Car, the most successful car rental company in the United States, measured in terms of revenues as well as customer satisfaction. Enterprise has built its business since 1957 with a singular focus on a specific customer problem—the need for a *replacement car.* The need can arise from a variety of reasons—perhaps the customer's car is being repaired or it's been in an accident or it's not suitable for a special occasion or whatever. This focus has led Enterprise to build 5,500 offices in neighborhoods across the United States and to position itself as the "neighborhood car rental company." While its competitors fight tooth and nail for the traditional business or leisure traveler who rents at the airport, Enterprise has captured a dominant share of the customers needing a replacement. Interestingly, the replacement car segment isn't the largest or even the most lucrative. But it's a segment that Enterprise's competitors are ill equipped to serve.

Partners: No company is an island, especially in today's connected and networked world. The partnerships and collaborative relationships that companies create to source, deliver, and add value to offerings can be a powerful lens for growth and competitive advantage. Partners can help companies to access capabilities, technologies, customers, or markets in ways they can't do alone. Partnerships are a particularly important lens for start-up companies looking to gain access to customers or for technology companies that want to harness the creative potential of developers to add value to their core offerings.

Mohan has been advising a start-up company called Georama that has created a one-stop solution for vacation travelers to plan, book, and share their trips on an interactive map. Georama's mission is to alleviate the pain of planning and booking leisure trips, which are often far less structured than business trips. While Georama's offering is innovative, it does not have the financial resources or the time to market its online travel solution to millions of leisure travelers. The key to its growth lies in its ability to develop partnerships with travel providers and online travel agencies that already have tens of millions of customers. For instance, Hilton Hotels has recently signed a deal with Georama to offer its trip planning service on Hilton's Web sites to the hotel company's customer base. This is a win-win partnership because the travel providers add value to their customers and generate more revenues from leisure trips, while Georama gets its offering in front of millions of customers that it did not have to acquire on its own.

Channels: The distribution channels are the routes that a company takes to get its offerings to market. These may include online channels, retailers, distributors, value-added resellers, brokers, kiosks, vans, or mobile channels. Channels can provide a powerful lens to focus a company's efforts to find innovative ways to get products to market. In emerging markets in particular, channels are a fertile ground for innovation and growth.

Consider how the Italian coffee maker Illycaffè SpA is focusing on a specific channel to grow its business in the United States. Traditionally, Illy has sold its coffee in the United States through high-end supermarkets and hotels. In 2008 the company began to expand its reach by doing distribution deals with independent diners and coffee shops—an effort to get its coffee in the hands of customers without having to build or operate its own outlets. Illy has created a program called *Artisti del Gusto* or Artists of Taste. Under this program, Illy supplies independent coffee shops with Italian espresso machines, coffee cups, and recipes. It also trains the shop employees. The coffee shops are then anointed as certified Illy providers, and they agree to serve Illy coffee exclusively. By replacing generic coffee with premium Illy coffee in white ceramic cups with the bright red Illy logo, the independent shops can increase the price of their coffee and generate more profits.

Markets: The many and various geographic markets often have different competitive environments, customer requirements, regulatory contexts, and distribution challenges. For instance, emerging markets differ in customers and infrastructure from developed markets. As companies search for focus, they might find that they are disproportionately well or poorly equipped to compete in specific markets. Hence, it's important to choose your markets well. For instance, Bahwan CyberTek, an IT services company that Mohan has been associated with since 2002, has focused on the Gulf and Middle East markets, most of which have monarchies, generate a significant proportion of their GDP from oil and gas, and require close relationships with key government decision makers. This focus has allowed the company to hone its offerings, its relationships, and its go-to-market strategy.

Monetization: At the end of the day, a company has to do more than create something of value—it has to capture some of the value for its employees and shareholders. It does that through the so-called monetization mechanism (also loosely referred to as the business model or the value capture). Stated simply, monetization mechanisms are the ways in which a company makes its money. Google makes most of its money from search engine advertising. Hewlett-Packard, for many years, made most of its money from printer ink. Business authors make their money from speaking and consulting, not from selling books.

In recent years, monetization mechanisms have become a powerful lens for growth and innovation. Consider the experience of EXLService (EXL), a business process outsourcing (BPO) and transformation services provider where Mohan has served on the board of directors since 2005. Traditionally, EXL gets paid on a time-and-materials basis. Clients pay a fee per FTE (full-time equivalent), called a "seat" in industry parlance. The problem with this monetization mechanism is that as EXL becomes more efficient at providing services, its revenues decline because it needs fewer seats for the same job. To remedy the situation, EXL created a new monetization mechanism called transaction pricing, under which EXL gets a specific fee per customer account. Clients appreciate that they get predictable billing. EXL likes being able to capture the economic benefits of increased efficiencies, offering a strong incentive to innovate. Transaction pricing has become a strong focus for EXL's revenue and profit growth, with more than 40 percent of its client revenues now converted to this new mechanism.

Processes: Business processes are the way work gets done in a company. These processes span various functions and entities, from customer management to supply chain to human resources, to name a few. Processes can become a powerful lens for focused growth and innovation, particularly in companies that have complex and expensive operations.

Lexus, the luxury division of Toyota, demonstrates the point in the way it manages the buying and ownership experience for its customers. When Lexus entered the market in 1989, the company did more than create a better car. It created an unparalleled end-to-end customer experience that begins with the purchase and continues with service and maintenance over the entire period that the customer owns the car. Lexus created attractive new dealerships, trained dealer employees to deliver a high level of service, provided loaner cars to customers and roadside assistance. Some dealers even offered champagne brunches to Lexus owners. By looking at car buyers through the lens of the customer experience process, Lexus became a leading luxury brand from a standing start. Today, competitors of Lexus, including Mercedes and BMW, have emulated several of the process innovations that Lexus brought to the market.

In summary, each of the eight lenses provides a way for companies to view the opportunity landscape in a focused manner. Each company has to evaluate what lens or set of lenses works best for its context. The exercise is to walk your way from lens to lens to see which opportunities come into focus.

BACK TO KRAFT

In early 2007, Kraft Developing Markets emerged from the discovery phase with an array of promising themes. Some things seemed pretty clear to all—the brand Tang, for example, despite problems, held enormous potential, in part because Kraft had built a successful brand over the decades and held a big advantage in the technology of producing powdered beverages—particle size, flavor, processing. Kraft's businesses in countries such as Brazil had developed a strong brand portfolio with world-class sales and distribution systems. Other workshop conclusions were more ambiguous. What to do with the Indian market, which had such great promise but had produced such limited results for Kraft over many years?

Over the course of a few weeks, a small leadership group, including Sanjay, met regularly to synthesize the material. What had genuine potential and what could be set aside? Which ideas could be grouped and refined? Which needed more research?

This was also the time to decide which existing initiatives or processes needed to be eliminated, curtailed, or modified. For example, Kraft's salty snacks businesses—potato chips and so on—were struggling in the Nordic countries. Was it worth continuing to fight for them? These businesses were soon sold.

As in the discovery process, the team drew on a handful of outsiders—investment bankers, consultants, suppliers, ad agencies—six or seven people who had been working with Kraft over the years and who brought their own points of view. Out of the round of meetings that followed, the group came up with a list of potential opportunities, which was circulated to the workshop participants for more feedback. Finally, the leadership team refined the list for going to the next stage: examining the opportunities through various lenses, from product categories to channels to new technologies, looking to highlight potential. On the technology front, for example, could Kraft scale up its leading-edge technology for making powdered beverages?

In the end, the group decided to emphasize three lenses—offerings (categories), brands, and markets. The choice was close to inevitable for a consumer products company, but the exercise of looking through other lenses helped in clarifying and spotting opportunities. The group also settled on numbers. From the sprawling operation, they would settle on five categories, ten brands, and ten markets. There was no real magic to selecting those numbers—they emerged simply because they were small, in keeping with the notion of focus, and distinctive.

The assignment now was to look through the lenses and find the products and places that made the cut.

THE THREE *MS*

3
Momentum
Margin
Materiality

The lenses help in illuminating particular aspects of the business and in pointing the way to potential big bets. But each lens may itself shine a light on several opportunities. These need to be prioritized according to three criteria, what we call the Three *M*s: Momentum (winning potential), Margin (profit potential), and Materiality (revenue potential). These criteria address three key questions that you need to ask in assessing an opportunity: Is it real? Is it worth it? Can we win?

Putting ideas through the screen of the Three *M*s allows the leadership to assess where the biggest opportunities are, where the company can make the most money, and where it has the best chances of topping the competition. Remember, ultimately, you are going to be distorting resources to channel them toward target areas of high potential. The objective at this stage is to settle on those target areas.

Here again, the research and discussion should be vigorous. How big is the potential payoff? What's the time frame? What resources would have to be poured into the effort? Every business will have its own decision-making criteria in sorting through the answers. What's important is that the discussion be informed and thorough.

Looking through the category lens at Kraft Developing Markets, for example, the leadership team held intense debates over whether chocolate and/or cheese should be among the five winners. The analysis followed the Three *M* formula, and here's how it unfolded. First, for chocolate:

1. *Momentum*—On the positive side, Kraft had a few businesses going in Europe, notably with great brands like Milka, and in Brazil, with the brand Lacta. There were synergies with cookies (biscuits), which had been identified as a priority category. The negatives were substantial: Past performance had been patchy. Chocolate was absent from many developing markets. Launch in these markets was possible but it would take effort and time to be material. Further, a lot of people thought the best opportunities had a health and wellness tilt, and chocolate is an indulgence. Finally, the barriers were relatively low—almost anyone could get into the chocolate game. What would be Kraft's point of differentiation?

2. *Margin*—The margins of the existing businesses weren't great. On the other hand, analysis suggested the margins could readily be improved through portfolio simplification, innovation, and cost reduction.

3. *Materiality*—In certain parts of the world, chocolate is a favorite treat—perhaps *the* favorite treat, so the potential looked good. But in many parts of the developing world—the anticipated source of a lot of growth—the sweet hadn't penetrated far. Then again, could an acquisition put Kraft in the game?

Given the analysis, the question was whether Kraft could make money and beat the competition in the category. Sanjay recalls that the call was close—it easily could have gone either way. What's key under Focus7 is to make a decision and make it quickly. Based on the Three *M* analysis, chocolate had strong enough potential to make the cut as one of Kraft's focus categories. The choice has paid off, as we'll soon see.

The leadership team went through a similar examination in considering the category of cheese:

1. *Momentum*—Kraft Macaroni & Cheese has reigned for years as a powerhouse brand in the United States. On the one hand, people argued that the consistent popularity of the product represented a point of difference—the brand was so strong. On the other hand, cheese is rare in most Asian diets. The challenge: Could Kraft teach people to like cheese? Probably, but it would take time.

2. *Margin*—The cheese margins were patchy wherever it was sold.

3. *Materiality*—If the upside approached the success of cheese in North America, Kraft would enjoy a revenue bonanza. However, reaching this upside would be challenging given the need to change the palates of Asian consumers who did not have a taste for cheese. How long would this take?

Again, the discussion was vigorous. In the end, the deciding factor proved to be momentum and the time and effort it would take. Yes, Kraft could introduce Macaroni & Cheese to the Asian markets, but customers would need to be educated about using cheese in their diets and in their recipes, an expensive process that would take years. Kraft could probably build a profitable business eventually, but only after enormous expenditures of time and money. Based on the momentum criterion, the Kraft managers decided to leave cheese off the list of priority categories for the time being—a difficult and controversial choice for Kraft, because the company had started out more than a century before as a cheese business, and many American consumers still thought of Kraft as the company that made Kraft Singles and Kraft Mac & Cheese. (Meantime, the company took a practical step by investing in cheese in select markets, such as Australia, where cheese was well established.)

Using a similar Three *M* analysis, the leadership ultimately decided that Ukraine belonged among the ten priority markets— the Kraft operation there was material and growing well, and, it was thought, the business there could be used as a spring-board to extend the business in the region. In a decision that startled a lot of people, India failed to make the list of priority markets. Tough choices have to be made. That is the essence of focus. Kraft's businesses in India were simply spinning too many wheels, going in too many directions, to gain sufficient momentum. The Kraft India business was deprioritized. A separate team was appointed to look at India fresh and con-sider investment only if Kraft could establish a profitable busi-ness model. Later, with the acquisition of Cadbury, Kraft had a significant enough presence in India that the country became a priority market.

Here's another example of focusing through a lens and then going through the Three *M* analysis: Fonterra Brands, the New Zealand dairy business where Sanjay worked before Kraft, owned a promising brand named Anlene, which in-cluded a range of products that help build and maintain strong bones. When a Fonterra leadership team considered the brand through the offering lens of medical expertise, Anlene stood out—its knowledge base and technology represented a strong point of difference at a moment when health care experts in-creasingly focus on osteoporosis. But the brand wasn't doing well. Except for some success in one or two countries, Anlene hadn't caught on with consumers. Still, looking at the business through the partnership lens, the leadership saw that in places where Anlene had established a foothold, Fonterra had worked with local health care operations.

On to the Three *M* analysis for Anlene:

1. *Momentum*—On the plus side, Fonterra had global expertise in healthy bones through Anlene, and the osteoporosis market was huge. On the other hand, despite various efforts in a number of countries, the Anlene products just hadn't caught on globally.
2. *Margins*—Where established, Anlene's margins were good.
3. *Materiality*—The brand's products held a technology advantage over rivals that had the potential to blossom into a huge success. On the other hand, the operation had remained small.

After considering the situation, Fonterra's leadership decided to bet on Anlene, promoting the brand through the fight against osteoporosis. But the initiative would start small—Fonterra would test the rollout and then build size if the results looked promising. Working with GE Healthcare's bone density technology and partnering with osteoporosis organizations, Fonterra set up the Anlene Bone Health Check, which provided free bone density screenings. The concept was tested at events around Asia, ultimately growing to screenings offered to millions of people in nine Asian countries. Anlene became a huge success with sustained profitable growth.

In all these instances, time is of the essence. Sanjay arrived at Kraft in January 2007 and Kraft Developing Markets unveiled its 5-10-10 focus in May, four months later. Leaders have to make choices, often without complete information and rarely with any certainty. And they need to make those choices fast. If you can get 80 percent of your strategy right, get going on it. You could spend additional months, or years, pushing to get the strategy to 90 percent right (no one gets to 100 percent), but then you've lost time and likely the opportunity. Even in selecting among opportunities, there may not be a single one that stands out—a perfect right answer. In fact, there may be several right answers, or, more precisely, several answers that can be made to work well. The key is to settle on your direction quickly, align around it, and then stick with it. As we will discuss later, the emphasis now needs to shift to execution.

By the end of this step of focusing through lenses and setting priorities, the team should have settled on several opportunities for each lens. These should be summarized in a simple preliminary plan—no more than one page. The document should be circulated among key stakeholders for further iteration. Move quickly, but allow the plan to go around several times, if necessary. Everyone needs to sign on and feel confident that he or she had a role in setting the direction.

You've now got a strategy—a plan to focus resources toward a select handful of initiatives. With that, you're ready to spread the word throughout the company.

STEP 2—STRATEGY:

PICK YOUR BETS

FIVE
KEY
TAKEAWAYS

1. To decide which growth opportunities to pursue, look at the opportunity landscape through lenses—dimensions on which a business is defined.
2. There are eight key lenses through which you can focus the analysis of opportunities: offerings, brands, customers, partners, channels, markets, monetization, and processes.
3. Choose a few lenses through which the most promising opportunities come into focus.
4. The opportunities highlighted through the lenses should

be evaluated based on three criteria, the so-called Three
Ms: Momentum, Margin, and Materiality.

5. In picking your strategy bets, don't expect to come up
   with the perfect strategy. If you can get it mostly right,
   move quickly and get started on execution.

CHAPTER 5

RALLYING CRY:
ROUSE THE TROOPS

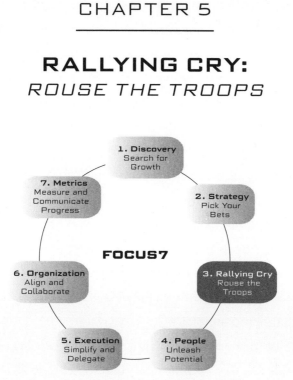

If you spill a handful of iron filings on a table, they will scatter into an unruly mess. But if you then pass over the mess with a strong magnet, the filings will arrange themselves into a regular order. A powerful rallying cry has the same effect on a company—working to bring employees, top to bottom, in line with the strategic direction of the business.

Under Focus7, once leaders have settled on the strategic direction, they must communicate the plan with a simple but compelling call to arms. That's the rallying cry, and it can come in various guises—a phrase, a number, an acronym, a symbol, an image. In one example we will discuss shortly, the rallying cry was incarnated successfully by a color.

A good rallying cry accomplishes a number of tasks, and the emphasis will vary based on the circumstances. As we will show, one type of rallying cry fits the situation where the company wants to hammer home newly defined business priorities. Another works best when leaders want to get employees emotionally charged behind a change in direction or a new way of looking at a brand. Yet another tries to raise aspirations and goals. Yet another is appropriate—most often in large service companies—when leaders want to convey guidelines on behavior to employees. In all cases, the message needs to be something basic and powerful that conveys meaning throughout the organization. There is no such thing as a rallying cry that is too simple!

Think of this step as a transition between strategy and action. You are descending from the somewhat abstract and rarefied air of planning to the concrete ground realities of execution, so you need the energizer that will make the strategy more concrete, more tangible, and more actionable. The rallying cry has to be connected to what people need to do. It needs to connect the boardroom with the people on the front lines, so that everyone understands his or her role in driving the growth strategy forward.

With the rallying cry launched, key players in the company should know the essential strategy. Question the leaders and managers, and they should be able to tell you how the organization has been focused to win. Without that knowledge, strategies and goals tend to get diluted and dissipated the further they get from the boardroom. Senior leadership has to make sure that the company and its employees are aligned. That's where the rallying cry comes in.

Finding the right message and spreading it to the troops requires care and insight, but it shouldn't take many months or years. As in all elements of Focus7, speed is a virtue. Possibilities should be explored, decisions made, and then the rallying cry should be launched with a memorable event to inspire the organization.

We should emphasize that the rallying cry doesn't always have to be a lofty slogan spread company-wide. Sometimes the target is just a unit or division, and the rallying cry applies to those workers only. On the opposite end of the spectrum, as we will show, sometimes the rallying cry can become part of the company's external advertising campaign.

In any case, the message should be consistent and reinforced across contact points. Within the company, leaders should take every opportunity to reiterate the rallying cry—at conferences, in literature, on coffee cups, T-shirts, signage, wherever. The reminders to employees should be everywhere. And this is important: The rallying cry can't just turn into marketing fluff—it needs to connect directly to strategy, and the leaders need to stand behind it.

One other key point: Stay the course. The rallying cry should not be changed every year or every time the leadership wants to shake up the organization. Too many companies keep piling on strategies. That only leads to confusion and distraction. Rather, the message needs to be in place for years. It takes time for employees to absorb the strategy and for it to work its magic. With a rallying cry sounded, the focus should turn to execution.

Based on our experience, we have identified five different types of rallying cries, each with a somewhat different effect: to enumerate, evoke, emote, elevate, and explain. Let's take a look at examples of these types and see how they were developed over the last decade or so at three companies where Sanjay has worked and two where Mohan has consulted.

RALLYING CRIES THAT ENUMERATE

This is one of the simplest examples because it deals with the dispersal of essential information—a basic but vital step. And this is where Kraft Developing Markets found itself in the spring of 2007. By then, as we've discussed, Kraft had gone through the first two steps of Focus7, discovery and strategy. These steps involved cocreation and the alignment of key leaders on where to focus. The leadership had settled on the plan to target five categories, ten brands, and ten markets, and the winning categories, brands, and markets had been selected.

At that point, Sanjay assembled a small team—himself and a couple of others who had been through the first two steps. They were looking for a rallying cry that would describe the strategy in simple terms that could be communicated widely so that everyone could execute within the agreed strategic framework. The team created a one-page document that explained the strategy of "Winning Through Focus," as it was called. And the document identified the five categories, ten power brands, and ten markets against which there would be an extraordinary distortion of resources. The new rallying cry would be 5-10-10. As basic as that.

The next step was to launch the program with a splash that would ripple throughout Kraft, so everyone got the message. Every big company has its own culture, its own way of organizing and of disseminating information. In this instance, Sanjay's team didn't want to introduce 5-10-10 as just another strategic initiative from corporate headquarters. The choreography of the presentation needed to be carefully arranged. So on an evening in May 2007, the top one hundred leaders of Kraft Developing Markets gathered on the ninety-ninth floor of what was then called the Sears Tower in Chicago (today the Willis Tower). The gathering started at five P.M. and the guests were greeted with cocktails. An air of celebration floated through the room. The event kicked off with awards. Though the business had struggled for years, there were pockets of success—as there always are—and various people and units were singled out for strong accomplishments. Lots of cheering and clapping—the idea was to set a winning tone. People are always more receptive when the environment is cheery.

After the awards played out, the gathering broke for fifteen minutes—the mood stayed high. When everyone reconvened,

Sanjay spoke. Most of the people there had participated in discovery workshops over the last few months, and Sanjay emphasized that he was summarizing the strategy that had been worked out by the group as a whole, that this was a product of input and discussion. They'd agreed to focus the company—and the strategy to get there was captured in the numbers 5-10-10. Now they would move toward execution and develop a road map to distort resources and focus them on the priorities. The focus strategy would be applied at the regional and country levels, with clear action plans and delineated roles at the local level, too.

Laminated cards featuring the 5-10-10 rallying cry and the chosen categories, brands, and markets sat on the tables around the room, one card for everyone. And with that, the event concluded, after barely an hour.

Country heads were sent off to spread the rallying cry to employees and to start putting the new strategy of "Winning Through Focus" into play. The leaders developed a guide that local managers could use to communicate the plan—again, it was contained in a single page. In the next one hundred days, each country developed its own road map on how to implement the strategy. The process again was to try to cocreate and align key stakeholders. We have found that engaging employees helps create stickiness for the strategy. The emphasis was on practical execution on the ground, with some clear metrics to monitor progress. While the rallying cry was announced in an hour, the message of 5-10-10 stayed consistent for years.

RALLYING CRIES THAT EVOKE

This type of rallying cry is more subtle, but it can be hugely effective and even fun, as shown by the experience of Unilever's Lipton, the best-selling brand of tea in the world.

Each year, the top one hundred or so executives from Unilever's tea-based beverages business from across the world gathered for an annual meeting to discuss the state of the business and the strategy going forward. In 1999, there was good news to report from Lipton, which was the most important business in the Unilever beverage portfolio—sales were strong and the innovation pipeline was full. But long-term problems persisted. Lipton's operations were fragmented around the globe, and the regional operations were poorly coordinated to capitalize on the brand's full potential.

In February that year, Unilever held the tea conference at Colworth House, a formidable eighteenth-century mansion set on lovely, grassy grounds in Bedfordshire, about sixty miles northwest of London. Unilever has owned the mansion for more than half a century and uses it as the centerpiece of a research facility.

The setting and the occasion combined to cast an air of serious purpose over the conference, the attitude that typically prevailed at these and similar Unilever meetings. But this time, as the Unilever and Lipton executives gathered to talk tea, stately Colworth greeted them with a shock: The entire lawn in front of the mansion shone in bright yellow. The grass had been dyed. Someone was sending a message.

In fact, a crew of workers had been out since early in the morning spraying the grass, while the organizers of the conference, the leaders of Unilever's beverages team, prayed that England's abundant rain would hold off. As it turned out, the weather cooperated and the beverages team indelibly imprinted on their colleagues the rallying cry that would lead a surge in international sales of Lipton Tea: "Paint the World Yellow with Lipton."

The yellow lawn helped kick off a new strategy. We discussed in chapter 3 how the discovery process had highlighted the consistent success of Lipton's tea business in Portugal and Saudi Arabia, where regional leaders had positioned their product to compete in the broader market of all beverages. At the same time, Lipton executives in both countries used the color yellow—the traditional color of Lipton packages—to show that Lipton was playing in the wider arena rather than in just the traditional tea market. In Portugal, among other initiatives, Lipton was showing itself on Portuguese beaches with yellow beach umbrellas, girls in yellow bikinis, and drinks being served in yellow mugs. Saudi Arabian managers opened Lipton Tea shops, casual drinking spots painted yellow throughout.

Regional executives in both countries had separately drawn upon a powerful psychological fact: Colors can evoke. Yellow signals sun, vitality, happiness, optimism. The associations abounded: Lipton brings brightness to your life. When you are down, it can lift you up. When you are up, it can calm you down. The color yellow casts a kind of aura, a compelling mixture of head and heart.

As Unilever's management looked at the Portuguese and Saudi Arabian operations, the brand's new strategy became apparent: Sell Lipton tea as not just a tea, but as the key ingredient of a pleasurable and healthy experience, an approach that would allow Lipton to operate in a wider beverages market, at the same time building on the core benefits of tea. Compared with coffee and colas, Lipton tea offered vitality and health. Using that strategy, Lipton could scale the successes of Portugal and Saudi Arabia across geographies.

Next, Lipton needed a rallying cry that would epitomize the strategy—something that would signal immediately and evocatively the new direction. Yellow was on everyone's mind, and soon a team of Unilever executives came up with "Paint the World Yellow with Lipton."

As it happened, Sanjay—the chief of Unilever's beverages category worldwide—had the assignment to organize the annual tea conference. He and his colleagues decided to use the Colworth House event to launch the new initiative. The arriving executives were used to being handed a folder of dry reports from around the world. The bright yellow lawn broadcast loud and clear that something new was under way.

The old chestnut that a picture is worth a thousand words rings entirely true when you are trying to evoke a reaction and an understanding that will stay in people's minds. Lipton wanted to imprint in its employees the experience they were now tasked to create, the new way of looking at tea. For something that elusive, that abstract, words may not be enough—visual expressions can have much greater impact. Hence, the yellow lawn.

Lipton's leaders codified the lessons learned from Portugal and Saudi Arabia. Phil Chapman, who worked with Sanjay for many years at Lipton (and later joined him at Kraft), put it memorably by announcing that Lipton's move into the wider beverages category was designed to increase the brand's SOB factor—share of bladder. Lipton operations in other countries were asked to implement a road map for execution. Internal communications highlighted successes and insights so best practices could spread. And Lipton kept spreading the color yellow to unify and excite its community of employees world-wide. This is a great example of: Find it. Bottle it. Scale it.

Meantime, to emphasize the change under way at Lipton, the leadership drew on two more visual signals that conveyed the message of change. A clip of Audrey Hepburn represented the old Lipton—classic, aristocratic, reserved. While a photo of Cameron Diaz—bright, sunny, vibrant—stood for the new business.

In the years following that conference, Paint the World Yellow became the backbone of an enormously successful Lipton marketing and business program that significantly accelerated growth of the company's tea business. Even in countries such as France that traditionally favor coffee, Lipton became hugely successful.

RALLYING CRIES THAT EMOTE

Fonterra Brands, where Sanjay worked before Kraft, faced a different sort of problem—it needed to connect its stakeholders, to pull a disparate, feisty group together. The best way to do that was to reach for their emotions.

A New Zealand cooperative owned by dairy farmers, Fonterra developed from the consolidation over the years of hundreds of smaller cooperatives and companies. Fonterra bills itself as the largest dairy exporter in the world. Sanjay arrived there in August 2004 as the managing director of the consumer and food service business. We have already discussed how the discovery and strategy steps led to the expanded success of Anlene, the bone health brand. Through the same two steps, Fonterra had also narrowed more than one hundred brands into a focus group of five and narrowed an array of markets into an emphasis on just a handful, while prioritizing channels such as food service. But discovery at Fonterra Brands also spotlighted trouble: The sprawling enterprise amounted to a landscape of operating silos with little cohesion. Strategy and goals for the company were all over the place.

What's more, the farmer-shareholders were a proud, independent bunch. They passionately believed in the value of what they were doing. Their dairy products provided the foundation of good health for millions of people. As the comment went, "If you cut a Fonterra farmer, he'd bleed milk, not blood." In line with the farmers' pride, the company was far ahead of the curve in the growing consumer focus on healthy living.

Fonterra needed a rallying cry that would pull these elements together with more than clever words and logic. What was needed was something that would convey the new strategy at the same time it connected emotionally with employees and, eventually, customers.

The company assembled a portfolio of images and phrases aimed at epitomizing Fonterra's direction. After just a few months, the Fonterra leadership made the call: Dairy for Life. The phrase captured two overlapping themes—the pride of the farmer-shareholders and the company's emphasis on natural products. And it perfectly hit that sweet spot between head and heart.

Given Fonterra's prior fragmentation, the new rallying cry was launched simply, with a small event at headquarters, and then phased in across the company. The slogan, rendered in soft blue and green, nature's colors, started appearing on letterheads, signs, business cards—gradually, all visual touch points would carry the slogan in the chosen colors. But the effort moved deliberately by design. In part that was simply practical—keeping costs in line as new communication materials were introduced across the company.

In both the Lipton and Fonterra examples, the company leaders weren't trying to set targets, though that would come later. With their rallying cries, they were trying to convey a renewed feeling or sense about a brand. Creating a Brand with Soul. Of course, this can be tricky territory. The rallying cry has got to mean something that is tacitly clear. If it's too vague, too abstract, too general, no one will get it. The Japanese have a word, *ba,* that means shared cognitive space, common cognitive ground. Even if the common ground can't be readily articulated, everyone involved implicitly understands what the point is. That's the quality Lipton and Fonterra reached for with Paint the World Yellow and Dairy for Life. They wanted to summon something that reached beyond targets and budgets. They wanted to persuade the employees and the farmer-shareholders that they weren't just working on a job, but that they were on a mission.

Brands with Soul go beyond just being products in a package—they combine functionality with a powerful emotional connection that, carefully nurtured, can live for generations.

RALLYING CRIES THAT ELEVATE

Sometimes an organization hopes to spur its people to think bigger, to elevate their aspirations. In those cases, rallying cries are usually framed in terms of targets.

Mohan sits on the board of Bahwan CyberTek (BCT), a privately held IT services company based in Oman and doing business in the Gulf, India, and the United States. Founded in 1999, BCT has grown steadily and in 2011 brought in about $100 million in revenues. Having gone through the strategy phase of Focus7, the leadership had decided to focus on four major markets—oil and gas, financial services, energy and utilities, and government. But as the management team got together in 2011, they realized that incrementalism had crept into the operation. The company was growing, but at a somewhat plodding pace—at the pace of a $100 million company. It all begins with aspirations. As it was, if the employees scored a $1 million contract, they thought it was a big win. They hardly even considered, say, a $10 million contract. But if BCT wanted to become a $1 billion company, its people top to bottom needed to start thinking like one. In short, they had to think big before they could get big.

So BCT's management team looked for a rallying cry to elevate aspirations. Putting their heads together, Mohan and the leadership team came up with 5x5 ("five by five"). The first 5 represented a growth target of five times $100 million in revenues or $500 million. The second five stood for five years (2011 to 2016). So the rallying cry challenged BCT to hit $500 million in revenues by 2016. This would mean growing the company almost fivefold. A tall order indeed!

Clearly, BCT wasn't going to reach that target by extrapolating from the current operations—growing steadily but linearly. The rallying cry forced everyone to work backward, so to speak, asking: If that's the target, what do we have to do to get there? It meant hiring people who could stretch and building products that will be the next generation. Passing up the marginal deals for the more ambitious contracts. Thinking bigger. (Always, of course, within the focus strategic framework.)

CEO S. Durgaprasad says the rallying cry has had a powerful effect on the company. "We have translated five by five down to what each business unit and each subsidiary of the company needs to do. Every member of the executive team has their marching orders and has developed plans for their role in achieving this ambitious target. There's a level of alignment and energy that we would never have had without this clear vision of where we need to get by 2016." BCT closed its 2013–14 fiscal year with $160 million in revenues, and it has successfully broken through the trap of incrementalism. While there is no guarantee the company will reach the 5x5 goal, it certainly wouldn't have come close to achieving what it has achieved to date.

RALLYING CRIES THAT EXPLAIN

Sometimes a company needs to raise a rallying cry to give its people a clear set of guidelines on what they are supposed to do and how they are supposed to behave. This holds particular relevance for big service companies with large contingents of relatively inexperienced workers. Leaders hope for a trickle-down effect—the standards trickle down to the cubicle, the call center, the checkout counter, wherever employees connect with customers.

McDonald's offers a prime example of a rallying cry that explains—one that has endured through more than half a century, almost since the moment Ray Kroc's enterprise began to expand across the country. The cry: QSC&V, representing quality, service, cleanliness, and value. Company history maintains that that acronym encapsulates Kroc's standards, which are applied to every restaurant and enforced through an intricate checking and grading system. Are the bathrooms clean? Was the order delivered on time? Was the food hot? And so on. What's more, those letters and the words they represent are drilled into every McDonald's employee.

Obviously, the cry was adopted long before Focus7 came into being. But the McDonald's story anticipates several of the elements of the Focus7 process. To start, the creators of the first restaurant, Dick and Mac McDonald, early on relied on focus, reducing the menu to a handful of items and recognizing speedy service as a core element in their success. And when the McDonald brothers' San Bernardino, California, restaurant caught the attention of Ray Kroc, he saw how the success could be scaled up, as long as the franchises stayed consistent in quality and style. That's where QSC&V came in.

If Kroc's standards helped launch the company, they are vital today to keep an enormous, sprawling operation on top of its game. McDonald's has more than 34,000 outlets in 119 countries and employs 1.8 million people. Many of those employees are new to the job and relatively inexperienced in any kind of work. Turnover is high. The rallying cry has to bring that huge workforce in line and implant those standards in everyone from the franchisee to the cook to the person handling drive-through orders.

Today, more than half a century after Kroc introduced QSC&V, the company continues to make the rallying cry a basic element in the training of every new employee and operator of a McDonald's restaurant. The cry—or its fundamentals— is continually reinforced in internal communications and on posters where McDonald's crews gather. Ask virtually any McDonald's employee about QSC&V, and chances are you would get a definition.

A rallying cry that explains works particularly well with a

large enterprise with many employees who deal directly with customers. This has been true for IndiGo, a low-cost Indian air carrier that was founded in 2006 and by 2013 had become the largest Indian airline by market share. More significantly, it has consistently shown a profit—a rarity among Indian carriers in the last few years. Like Spirit Airlines, IndiGo's success stems from its relentless focus on its low-cost niche. That focus has been encapsulated and spread company-wide by a rallying cry (with some small variations) that crisply articulates Indi-Go's vision: On Time, Low Fares, Hassle-Free. The IndiGo team knows exactly what this rallying cry translates into—processes and rules that are safe and simple, that make sense, and that cut waste and hassles, which in turn ensures a uniquely smooth, seamless, precise, gimmick-free customer experience at fares that are always affordable. On an IndiGo flight from New Delhi to Bangalore recently, Sanjay tested the power of the rallying cry by asking a flight attendant about it. She could articulate the three-point strategy exactly.

CONNECTING INSIDE AND OUT

Rallying cries begin inside the company by energizing employees, but they then need to be transmitted outside the company. Think of the rallying cry like the ripples that move ever outward when a pebble is dropped into water. Its influence needs to spread from employees to the company's partners and channels and ultimately to its customers around the world.

In the case of Fonterra, the internal rallying cry eventually moved unchanged into external marketing. Bahwan CyberTek's 5x5 obviously won't turn into a marketing slogan, but the internal message should push the company to take on the characteristics of a bigger operation and hence change the way customers and potential customers view it. Kraft's 5-10-10 funneled attention toward those selected brands and elevated their profile among consumers. QSC&V should redound to the advantage of everyone who buys a McDonald's hamburger—and thus improve the chain's competitive edge.

The point is to think through how the rallying cry is going to connect to every touch point at which you interact with customers. Your business only exists because of them.

STAYING ON POINT

We have given examples above of how leaders can spread the idea of the rallying cry to the troops—training, messages, rallies, signage, and so on. But it's worth emphasizing again the role the rallying cry should play. It is the manifestation of the strategy. For leaders and managers the rallying cry should be a lodestar, a constant reference point, and all significant decisions should link back logically to it. This takes discipline and frequent questioning: How does this step connect to the overall strategy?

A few years ago, Mohan experienced a telling example of how Starbucks had infused every employee with the purpose and direction of the company. In the early 2000s, Starbucks was on a growth tear, driven by its ambition to become a brand that is ubiquitous in its presence. The company expanded into seemingly every street corner, grocery store, airport, and office building. But this "Starbucks everywhere" wasn't just an abstraction. The strategy trickled down to low-level employees on the front lines. One day Mohan wandered into the marketing department supply room at the Kellogg School of Management and came across a man from Starbucks installing a coffee machine. The man explained that Starbucks was providing the machine free—the coffee company would get its return selling beans to the marketing department. "You can have Starbucks coffee right in your office," the man said.

That set Mohan to thinking: He could venture downstairs to the building cafeteria and buy a cup of Starbucks, but he'd pay close to two dollars. If he wanted a fancier brew, he could walk to the Starbucks café across the street and pay $3.25 for a grande latte. So he asked the Starbucks installer, "How much do you make on a cup worth of beans?"

"About 18 cents here," the man said.

Mohan pounced: "You guys are foolish. Why cannibalize $2.00 or $3.25 with 18 cents?"

The man was unflappable. "How many cups of coffee do you drink in a week?" he asked. "And how often do you just grab a coffee from the supply room and not go downstairs or across the street?"

Mohan estimated that he drank five to ten cups a week, and

that about half the time he's too pressed to do anything but grab a cup from the supply room.

The Starbucks man explained patiently, "When you grab a quick cup of coffee here, it is 'convenience.' When you go down to the cafeteria, it is a 'break.' When you go to Starbucks with a friend, it is 'socialization.' These are three distinct consumption occasions. They don't cannibalize each other! We at Starbucks want one hundred percent 'share of your stomach.'"

The business professor realized he had just received a vivid lesson in the power of permeating a company with a basic strategy—everyone, from the CEO to the barista to the installer, could understand, articulate, and put the plan into action.

With focus like that, top management can get down to the business of making smart bets on people and ideas.

STEP 3—RALLYING CRY:

ROUSE THE TROOPS

1. Business leaders may define strategy, but it needs to be implemented by people. To convert strategy into action, create a rallying cry—a hook that articulates the strategy and aligns people behind it.
2. The rallying cry can be a phrase, a color, a number, an acronym, a symbol—something simple yet vivid that brings the strategy to life for everyone in the organization.
3. Rallying cries serve five sometimes overlapping purposes— to explain, enumerate, emote, evoke, and elevate.

4. Rallying cries can be applied at different levels in a company, from a business unit to the entire organization.
5. Rallying cries should be created quickly but maintained for a long time because the message takes a while to seep into the organization.

CHAPTER 6

PEOPLE:
UNLEASH POTENTIAL

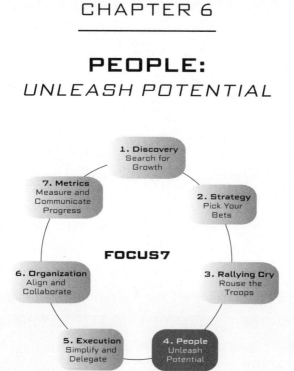

With the strategy defined and the rallying cry in place, the next step in Focus7 is to find and empower the people who can make growth happen. Getting the best out of people is one of the essential tasks for a business leader. Harry Kraemer, the former CEO of Baxter International and now a faculty colleague of Mohan's and Sanjay's at the Kellogg School of Management, summed up his approach to leading people in simple terms:

"Find the right people. Put them in the right jobs. And get the hell out of the way!"

Kraemer's comment captures some of the key elements of dealing with people in the Focus7 framework. Identify the few high-potential people who can drive the growth initiatives. Give them disproportionate responsibility and resources. Then step back as they go beyond the call of duty and deliver results that you or even they considered impossible.

How do you recognize those special people? Usually, they've got four essential qualities. One is *passion*—they find real purpose in what they do and devote unbounded energy to it. They don't look at their job as a Monday to Friday, nine-to-five obligation, but as an adventure, even a game, with highs and lows, triumphs and setbacks. Their work engages their interest and imagination, which in turn fuels their energy.

The high performers also understand the value of working on a *team*. They collaborate easily. They find the ideas and contributions of others stimulating, not threatening.

The best are also *transformational*—call them transformers. They identify issues and are eager to solve them. They make changes, not for the sake of change, but because they see that things can be better and they've got the spirit and energy to tackle the problem. Their bias is to get things done. In a good way, these restless revolutionaries are often permanently *dissatisfied*. They are not whiners, but their antennae are constantly picking out ways their world can be better.

High performers of this sort exist in almost every company, but in large corporations they often get buried inside the byzantine organizational maze. The job of a leader is to find them and turn them loose. The same ideas that apply to strategy in Focus7 apply to people—bet on fewer people. Bet bigger on them. And be bold in letting them run with their dreams. "Look for the person with passion and energy and a drive for accomplishment," says Kraft's Pradeep Pant. "You won't go wrong."

Of course, you need to maintain a balance—every business needs the solid types, the nuts-and-bolts folks who can get things done. These are dedicated managers and workers who aren't going to start a revolution, but they understand the business and work hard at it. They take on a critical role in executing the strategy.

For all these players, working together is a key. The leaders across divisions and units have got to know they are operating as a family. Interdependence and give-and-take counts for all. Each leader has to balance the good of his or her unit with the larger good of the company.

The logic is basic: In today's connected world, collaborative networks trump the soloist (a point we will return to in chapter 8). We have all witnessed examples of brilliant performers who enjoy spikes of success, but no one wants to work with them. They don't accept or understand the importance of co-creation. While there are valuable roles for people of that sort, the soloist typically won't ignite the creativity, excitement, and devotion of colleagues, which is where the true potential lies. That hoary elementary school evaluation—"Works well with others"—resounds with relevance in the grown-up world of business today.

One valued characteristic that sometimes gets overlooked—particularly in large companies with well-drawn lines of authority—is candor. At its best, candor represents an array of qualities founded on straight talk and straight thinking. It's easy to hide behind a PowerPoint presentation—the people with the confidence and informality to step out and speak directly to the facts are keepers.

Sanjay experienced a vivid example of this shortly after he joined Kraft. He was visiting Kraft's Chinese office in Beijing, and the regional leadership team had planned a lengthy presentation for their new boss on the state of the business. Mark Clouse, at the time head of Kraft China, met Sanjay at the Beijing airport and rode with him back to the office. During the hour's drive, Sanjay asked Clouse for a briefing on the business, and that set off a frank and thorough discussion. There was both good and bad news to report, and Clouse did more than simply lay out the situation—he had a clear plan of action. "We literally did my annual budget in the car, and we aligned on numbers," Clouse recalls. "I talked about the issues and we talked about what we needed."

When they reached the Beijing office, Sanjay hopped out and announced that since he now knew where things stood, it was time to get down to the job of moving forward. The leadership team was stunned—they'd planned three hours of reports and slides.

Clouse's approach exactly captured the spirit of *Karna Kya Hai?*—"*So what do we do now?*" His candor inspired trust in his colleagues and his bosses. It hardly needs saying that he moved up in the organization quickly and became president of North America for Mondelēz International.

If you are launching an effort to transform or reenergize your business, sometimes you will have to look outside. When Lipton launched its Paint the World Yellow strategy, the company aimed to succeed in the wider market of beverages, not just in tea. Lipton wanted to move sales beyond grocery stores and into consumption outside the home. But the company, while strong in grocery skills, lacked depth or experience with other distribution channels and with beverages besides tea. To augment the existing team, Lipton hired twenty-five managers from beverage companies—a key step on the way to building a cadre of Paint the World Yellow missionaries.

A merger or acquisition can pose other problems—in particular, a potentially crippling anxiety among workers. Who will be in charge? Will some be let go? The concerns are completely understandable. In such a situation, leaders must move quickly. They need a plan for integration, and they need to stay focused on what matters—merging the operations with as little disruption as possible.

When Kraft acquired Cadbury in 2010, the two companies had overlapping operations in scores of countries. To reduce anxiety, Sanjay and his team decided to settle on a single leader and leadership team for each country within a hundred days. Then Kraft put to work an outside agency to assess who had the best skills to go with each position.

The process moved swiftly and it was fair—more important, it was seen to be fair by leaders at both Kraft and

Cadbury. "We were dealing with two big and very proud companies and initially there was a lot of opposition to the merger," says Tim Cofer, who did a brilliant job heading the integration team. "Getting the right people in the right roles quickly made a big difference in the success of the integration."

In retrospect, the personnel selections probably came out about 80 percent right—a success rate that's fine, because what's important is to make selections that are broadly successful and settled quickly so the merged companies can get on with the business of transformation. Adding time to the decision process probably won't make a meaningful difference in the outcome.

In keeping with our bias for action, a tight timetable also helps with the ongoing process of identifying up-and-coming talent. Smart leaders are always thinking ahead and recruiting ahead of a specific need. If someone of great talent and skills appears on the radar screen, try to find a place for him or her. One superb talent is worth ten average performers.

With the key players assembled and the strategic framework in place, you are ready to move forward—making the fewer, bigger, and bolder bets.

DISTORTING RESOURCES

The logic of a focused operation rests on the simple premise that you reallocate resources toward the areas of the business where you have the best chances to win. But resources—money and talent, particularly—are finite. That means you need to take from areas that are not priorities and give to areas that are. We call this distorting resources and it applies to people, to funding, and to the way senior managers allocate their time. Once Kraft introduced 5-10-10, for example, Sanjay only visited the top ten markets and spent virtually all his efforts on the ten focus brands. But even then he had to manage his time carefully—distorting attention among the focus brands according to priorities and initiatives.

When it comes to money, the task is to reshape the budget. The leadership has to be disciplined and rely on the power of saying no. Funding needs to be moved from nonfocus areas. Some projects can be stopped entirely. Others can be delayed. This can get painful. When it comes to marketing a beloved but pokey brand, historic levels of spending get cut. The money goes toward an initiative with more potential. Favorite projects get starved. And nothing is static. Funding decisions evolve with circumstances. A sudden and unforeseen change in the business may require more distortion, more squeezing from noncore projects. Managers have to remain nimble and disciplined.

But let's be clear: This is part of the job description of every business leader. This is what he or she has been hired to do. The difference is the clarity of purpose and the pace of decision making. Distorting resources can't be pushed back to the next budgeting cycle. Choices have to be made now.

Many of those choices can be guided by the continuous

demand to cut costs and simplify. Layers of management, administrative overheads, products with low margins—every aspect of the business needs to be scrutinized regularly, looking to streamline or eliminate, freeing up resources to steer toward the priorities. The goal of Focus7 is to create growth that raises the gross margin and sustains itself. Those improved margins should throw off more money that can be tapped to invest behind priorities. That's the payoff of distorting resources.

Under the right circumstances, you can take the idea of distorting resources to an even higher level—firing up one of the most powerful though counterintuitive tools in the Focus7 program.

THE BLANK CHECK

			Date: Today
Pay to the order of:	**Blank Check**	$	
You write in the amount you need!		Dollars	
Memo		*Sanjay Khosla*	

A decade ago, Kraft was facing a major challenge with Tang— the powdered breakfast drink that had long been one of its iconic brands. After rocketing to fame, literally, as a drink carried by U.S. astronauts in the 1960s, the brand had fallen into a cycle of underperformance. Around the globe, Tang's managers launched a number of initiatives, but the innovations were either off target or amounted only to small steps. In Latin America, for example, where the volume of sales at least remained steady, Tang's managers tried producing a bottled, ready-to-drink version, and even experimented with Tang yogurt. "We were actually losing focus on what the main attributes of the brand were delivering," recalls Gustavo Abelenda, president of Kraft Latin America.

Nonetheless, in 2007 Tang made the list as one of the top ten focus brands in 5-10-10. Despite its troubles, leadership recognized that Tang had the Three Ms. Even with its flattening performance, the business had materiality—almost $500 million in annual sales outside the United States. The margins were good. And Tang had the potential to pick up momentum. The brand had recognition worldwide. Its powder technology surpassed rivals. And it was on trend—because it's easy to transport and relies on water, Tang is one of the greenest beverages on the market. But how could Kraft reignite the old favorite? Kraft adopted a bold strategy for boosting sales back into the stratosphere: Tang leaders in key countries were told to dream big and not worry about resources. Mark a huge goal and go for it.

So they did—in ways we will describe below. The results were outstanding. In five years, Tang doubled sales and became a $1 billion brand—after taking nearly fifty years to reach the $500 million revenue mark.

The secret of Tang's turnaround was what we call a blank check—a deal that freed the Tang team from the sorts of resource anxieties that could limit innovation. In effect, the deal said: Forget about the budget—if the Tang team comes up with a plan with a good chance to supercharge sustainable growth, Kraft will pay for it. This, of course, contradicts a line of business gospel: Live within your means. Managers have always been taught that they have to work with the limited resources available. Unfortunately, resource constraints limit more than plans. They also limit the creative potential of people.

We have found that if you take away the inhibitions imposed by budgets and other resource restrictions, people think differently—they address problems with a fresh eye, they become more entrepreneurial, their imaginations soar. Put another way, people lose their fear of failure. "It's almost like the Wizard of Oz giving the Scarecrow a diploma or the Cowardly Lion a medal," says Carlos Abrams-Rivera. "You are giving people a signal to stop being afraid, because in fact they are afraid—they have learned the right business models, so they are."

Here's what we propose: Under the right circumstances and within the strategic framework, leaders should focus on defining ambitious goals and leave it to their managers and their teams to ask for *whatever resources they need* to achieve these goals. When teams decide their own budgets, they act as owners—in our experience, it's remarkable how often they are inspired to achieve outstanding results.

Kraft Developing Markets started issuing blank checks in

2007. Five years later, the company ran an assessment of how the initiatives had worked. Seventy percent had succeeded. But even taking into account the failures, the blank-check initiatives far outperformed regular operations.

A word of clarification: A blank check can be a powerful tool under the right circumstances, but it should be used selectively—it is not the operating mechanism for the company as a whole. For example, only a few of the ten brands singled out in 5-10-10 were targeted directly for blank checks—though all received focused attention and resources. Leaders need to keep running all other aspects of the business as the opportunities to use blank checks unfold.

Blank checks are a metaphor for the freedom given a team to determine for itself the resources needed to meet agreed-upon goals within a defined time frame. Blank checks exhort teams to shoot for the moon, while giving them the rocket fuel they need to break free of the gravitational pull of predetermined budgets and business as usual. But blank checks are not a license to spend without limits, without guidelines, or without consequences. Teams have to define the resources they need—they must fill in the amount of the blank check. Every blank-check initiative needs to be consistent with the company's overall business strategy. And it needs to have the potential to produce sustained, profitable growth.

Blank checks are not meant to produce one-hit wonders that bring a short-term spike in results. The idea of the blank check is to empower big ideas that drive a virtuous cycle and change the business's trajectory for the long term.

Teams that sign up for blank checks are held strictly account-able for quantifiable results. Blank checks represent freedom within a framework—freedom to act, but with a set of ground rules to ensure that the initiatives stay on strategy and produce results. For example, the framework might include the company focus areas, as with 5-10-10. The framework might reflect the deployment of innovation platforms. The point is—and this is crucial to keep in mind—the blank-check initiative should align with the settled direction of the company.

Blank checks need not be applied only against growth op-portunities. They are equally applicable against cost saving programs or in improving productivity. Teams are given extra-ordinary resources and attention to achieve ambitious goals even if it means making heavy investments in the short term.

HOW BLANK CHECKS WORK

To put the blank-check idea to work, business leaders need to go through a systematic process of picking the best bets, se-lecting the team, defining goals and plans, kicking off the ini-tiative, and monitoring the results. Here's what happens at each of these five steps.

1. Picking the best bets. Blank checks are designed to fund big bets, so the bets have to be chosen carefully.

As the business leaders look for targets, they need to keep in mind the Three Ms. The blank-check initiative should in-volve an aspect of the business that has significant momentum. These bets aren't Hail Mary passes—they are smart plays that draw on the company's strengths. Margin potential continues to be important. Cost and price structures of the initiative need to remain competitive. This is particularly true in ventures in developing markets. You have to benchmark against the best out there, which often means the local competition. And the venture should be material—something that produces high impact with the least possible effort. If the only hope is to get small results relative to the company's size, why waste your time? It contradicts the whole notion of focus. There should be sufficient headroom for the business to grow.

"This is a bet you're making knowing that you have big odds in your favor," says Shawn Warren, who served as president of Kraft China. "The Three Ms have to line up and you've got to have a strong team to make it work."

2. Selecting the team. Blank checks are ultimately big and bold bets on a few people, rooted in the faith that they have the potential, the passion, and the perseverance to transform their businesses. Top leadership selects the team leader, and, obviously, the person drafted has to know the area of the business for which the blank check is to be issued. But the team leader need not be the most senior or most experienced manager in the area—more important is for him or her to have the most potential. And that is just the initial criterion.

The business leaders must ask themselves a series of questions about the blank-check candidate. Is this person a natural choice for the challenge based on his or her current responsibilities and span of control? Will this person be willing to take on the responsibility and not be frozen by fear? Is this person capable of thinking in new ways? Does this person have the capacity to inspire others to do things differently? Does this person have a track record of delivering results?

In both assessing potential team leaders and identifying likely initiatives, a useful analytical tool is to ask the candidate: If you had no constraints whatsoever and all the resources in the world, what's possible with this business? How high could you go? The answer can tell you a lot about the creativity and gumption of the person asked—and also provide clues to areas of the business that hide real potential.

Picking the blank-check team leader marks the first step in assembling a team. Then the leader works with the wider organization to put together a small group with the range of skills necessary to give the initiative every chance of success. Identifying the required expertise can be a rolling process as the effort moves forward. When various projects are developed, new needs will be recognized and the team can evolve accordingly. Sometimes the team will need to hire external expertise, and, in fact, an outsider's perspective can serve as a helpful stimulus.

Depending on the circumstances, members of the team could hold down their regular jobs while following through on the blank-check initiative. But here's where resource distortion comes into play. Running a blank-check initiative will be taxing in time and effort. The overall leadership has to provide the backup help on regular operations to give the blank-check team members the freedom to devote to this special assignment.

3. Defining goals and plans. Once the leadership has selected a likely initiative and assembled the team that will receive the blank check, the business leaders need to define the goals they expect the team to achieve. Goals need to be quantified, aggressive, and time-bound. Quantified goals are unambiguous—everyone understands them. Goals should be measurable on well-defined metrics, such as revenues, gross margins, and cash flow. And the goals need to be aggressive—they can't be reached simply by making incremental improvements. The idea is that the goals are stunning enough to force the blank-check team to question all assumptions about the business and to confront orthodoxies that have been blindly accepted by the company.

In the case of Tang, for example, Kraft Developing Markets leadership issued a dramatic challenge: Double sales in five years. After Kraft bought Cadbury, the goal for India came with a harsh deadline: Make India a half-billion-dollar business by the end of the year—which meant accelerating the region's total sales by 25 percent in ten months.

Blank-check initiatives should be guided by short deadlines, usually limited to a few years at most, and the goals should be set out on an even shorter time frame—six months or twelve months—so progress can be closely tracked. The pressure forces the team members to produce results quickly. They do not have the luxury of pursuing marginal improvements or initiatives that will take years to show results, and they will have the knowledge to make the necessary course corrections early on.

The typical first reaction to a blank-check challenge is skepticism. People in corporate settings have been conditioned to fight for every resource. Indeed, it is shocking to see the amount of energy expended in many companies just making things happen internally or pleasing the boss rather than focusing externally. Employees have been trained to think in terms of budgets, cost cutting, and belt tightening. They have likely never been in a situation in which they can ask for unlimited resources, and they may find the idea so foreign that it is difficult for them to believe it at first. Once the team realizes that their business leaders are serious, skepticism can easily give way to fear—fear of failure and fear of being in the spotlight.

Company leaders should do their best to reassure—the blank check represents a compliment, a sign of trust. What's more, the blank-check leader has been handed a huge opportunity, both to grow the business and to shine personally. Success is expected, but not a given, and failure will not be punished. Bonuses will be protected regardless.

Fear is often followed by frenetic activity, when the blank-check team tends to focus on doing more of the same or doing the same things better. But the team quickly realizes that this linear and extrapolative thinking will not produce breakthrough results. This, in turn, leads the team to powerful insights.

George Zoghbi was part of a team at Fonterra Brands that was handed a blank check in 2004 to bolster Fonterra's lagging food service business. "Oh, you feel a huge weight of responsibility just descended on you," recalls Zoghbi, who later became president of cheese at Kraft Foods. "You feel the person [writing the blank check] has blind trust in you—'I can't let him down'—and your level of accountability will increase at a phenomenal rate."

The team works under a tight deadline for coming up with

a plan. The short time frame signals that the challenge is not part of the normal course of business and prevents the team from becoming paralyzed by overanalysis. On the other hand, smart analysis sits at the heart of the potential plan, which needs to find a way to change the trajectory of the business while sticking to prudent business decisions.

In the Fonterra case, Zoghbi's team formulated a three-part plan—to focus strictly on those dairy products that had potential to grow fast and profitably; to augment skills by hiring people who had food service expertise; and to stay highly entrepreneurial when the results started coming in, pushing successes and pulling back on products and initiatives that didn't accelerate.

Having settled on its plan, the blank-check team should submit a short business proposal that reflects the Three *M*s. The proposal needs to define the initiative and the key steps in producing the agreed-upon results. Specificity counts. Zoghbi's team, for example, listed the products targeted for emphasis, the key customers, and the key markets. The proposal should include the goals, the time frame, steps detailing how the plan will be executed, key milestones and deliverables, and financial projections.

Along with the proposal, the team also has to fill in the amount of the blank check—the funding they seek. Over the years, we've been associated with blank checks that have ranged from a few million dollars to many millions. The amount should be more than enough for the team to carry out the initiative without worrying about running out of money. And the blank check doesn't concern money alone—people with special skills can also be part of the request.

The ultimate decision on green-lighting rests with company leadership. The review should be rigorous and quick. The process is undergirded by one word—trust. The leadership trusts the blank-check team to bring in a success. Senior leadership should stay out of the way.

4. Kicking off the initiative. Once the business plan has been agreed upon, company leadership formally issues the check by approving the amount and transferring the first round of funding into an account that can be accessed by the team leaders.

Where do the resources come from? More distortion—in fact, blank checks usually represent distortion of previous distortion. The leadership's decisions don't get any easier. The endeavor is constant—continuous simplification of how work is done. Stopping or curbing nonpriority initiatives. Aggressive programs to keep costs low. There is no magic fund to tap for blank checks. All resources are finite.

Mark Clouse, who moved from Kraft China to Kraft Brazil, recalls the effort to find funding for blank-check projects: "In Brazil, we had a grocery business that was gelatins, baking powders, just a bunch of odds and ends, and we continued to support it because the margins were good. But there was never a potential for a major contribution. So we completely retooled it—we made it a small shop, a few people. We gave them the right approaches and said, 'Look, just hit your numbers, but don't bother with the rest of the business.'"

The money from that grocery business—as well as from other nonpriority items and significant cost reductions—was deployed toward priority brands, such as Tang, and put behind other blank checks.

Remember also that the blank check can be drawn on resources in general—not simply money. So the blank-check team should be free to ask for people, skills, corporate attention, whatever is needed to make the goal.

5. **Monitoring results.** As the blank-check initiative begins, it is important to set milestones for key deliverables and then to monitor them closely. We recommend quarterly milestones, so that course corrections can be made quickly.

We will deal more specifically with metrics in chapter 9, but suffice it to say that the metrics for blank-check initiatives should be kept simple enough that progress can be measured on a single-page report. If we are dealing with product sales, we generally like to see sales/market share, margins, and cash flow.

Like the typical business start-up, blank-check initiatives rarely go according to plan. The team will run experiments and take risks, and some of these experiments will inevitably fail. Failing is part of the learning process. As we will discuss shortly, what is important is to fail early, fail cheaply, and learn fast. But running a blank-check initiative provides the kind of learning-by-doing experience that becomes a far more effective teaching tool than all the lectures and PowerPoint presentations from the big bosses.

HOW BLANK CHECKS DRIVE GROWTH

To see how blank-check initiatives work in practice and the results they can produce, let's take a closer look at three recent Kraft initiatives in developing markets: the revitalization of Tang, the acceleration of the Cadbury business in India, and the transformation of Kraft in China.

DOUBLING THE TANG BUSINESS IN FIVE YEARS

The developing markets leadership team issued a blank check to a team of Tang leaders in key global markets, asking them to connect locally with consumers, while leveraging the resources of the $50 billion global Kraft Foods organization.

First, Sanjay and the other leaders chose Alejandro Lorenzo, the head of Tang in Brazil, to lead the blank-check team. Lorenzo enjoyed strong credentials for the role—he knew the business, he had energy and drive, and he had a history of working well as part of a team. Still, Tang was floundering in Brazil and elsewhere.

With a blank-check leader in place, Sanjay sat down with Lorenzo and several regional leaders, including Mark Clouse and Gustavo Abelenda, president of Kraft Latin America. Today, Lorenzo remembers that meeting as painful. "We had to face the truth," he recalls. Sanjay got right to the point: Tang was going nowhere, the brand was wallowing in mediocrity. Then Sanjay gave them that staggering target: Double the business in five years. He promised a blank check to get there, but they had to come back with something inspiring and exciting. They had complete freedom. The timetable? Bring back your thoughts in four weeks.

"I was flabbergasted," recalls Lorenzo. "But after I picked myself up off the floor, I realized that to get to that target we were going to have to change our approach entirely."

The message was clear: This was not business as usual. In four weeks, Lorenzo and his team returned with some initial plans, but more important they asked for resources—not so much money at this point, but people with particular skills. So another five or six Kraft people from around the globe joined the blank-check team, including marketing and packaging experts. Lorenzo also hired two external agencies for marketing and analytical help. For another couple of weeks the group worked the phones and e-mail, churning through ideas. Sanjay didn't give them any guidance—he readily acknowledged that he didn't have a clue how they would reach the goal. If there was any doubt, that confession drilled home the point to all: Senior people don't have superior knowledge.

So what do they have that makes them effective leaders? Often, the best role of senior management is to create an environment where creativity flourishes and mechanisms like blank checks are instituted to unleash the potential of people.

After four weeks, Alejandro Lorenzo's team came back with a broad plan and preliminary budget request. Kraft had asked for something that would start showing results within twelve months. The team raised the pressure. Tang's sales peaked in the warm season, which was the December–March quarter in most regions where Tang sold well. That meant the new program had to be up and running within nine months or so.

Faced with that timetable, the blank-check team had realized that it needed to go to the core of the business. Tang came in a variety of flavors, but Tang Orange accounted for more than half of sales. That's where the effort should focus if they were going to drive immediate results. The team came to realize that Tang's managers had been trickling away energy and resources on a large number of small things—yogurt Tang, bottled Tang. Those innovative initiatives drew lots of attention and excitement, but they didn't pay off well. Lorenzo's team closed them down. Meantime, Tang Orange would get star focus. Tang's managers would rally the sales force behind that iconic drink. They'd generate news in the marketplace—create consumer contests, reignite the merchandising, improve displays, install sales incentives. On this element, the team had turned to the familiar, but they sensed that that was where they would get the bang for the buck.

Two other elements of the team's plan were more unusual. First, there had been talk for years of innovating Tang's packaging, in particular creating a one-drink-size sachet—something that would reduce the price point, ease sampling, and make the product generally more fun. The blank-check team brought on a Kraft packaging expert, João Moreira, of the Latin America regional office, and set him to work.

Moreira quickly made contact with an Italian company named Boato Pack that was pioneering machines for packaging. Boato came up with a prototype of a one-serving sachet of Tang. Moreira showed it to Alejandro Lorenzo and Mark Clouse. They got excited. They showed it to Gustavo Abelenda, who was about to fly to a leadership meeting in Chicago. Abelenda took a sample sachet along and in the middle of the meeting pulled it out of his pocket. The leadership team gave the green light on the spot. No one knew for sure whether the investment would pay off, but the leaders read the excitement and trusted the blank-check team.

The second unusual feature of the initial blank-check proposal counts as unusual only because it is so often overlooked. Faced with the fierce goal and deadline, the team revisited fundamentals, relying on workshops and research. "This sounds very basic, but we needed to understand clearly what consumers wanted—and that was a good, fruit-flavored product with high quality and convenience, at an affordable price," says Abelenda. "Once we had that insight, it was very easy to elaborate the vision."

Based on that insight, the team decided to up the ante on Tang's environmental advantages and its healthful side—a heritage going back to the astronauts, for whom Tang was a source of vitamins. This meant taking direct aim at rival beverages and making the most of what some regarded as a handicap. "Over the years, more and more meals had been converted into carbonated soft drink experiences instead of Tang," recalls Mark Clouse, who became president of North America for Mondelēz International. "And, to be fair, Tang really had become fairly boring. It was very heavy on a nutrient bundle—almost a medicinal cocktail."

So the team came up with a marketing solution that aimed

straight at the most important consumer: children. "Tang has a very powerful sustainability underpinning because of its connection to fresh water and the minimal packaging and energy used to make it," Clouse says. "We'd also learned that kids in Brazil were frustrated about not being taken seriously. So we created what we called the Kids Movement around Tang based on the idea of owning the planet."

We will consider the execution of these plans in detail in the next chapter, but the Tang case illustrates several insights about blank checks. The aggressive target forced the team to realize that the strategy in place—the incremental innovations— would not be enough. They also realized, as teams frequently do when taking on a blank-check challenge, that they did not have all the answers. They reached out to different types of outsiders, including packaging experts, supply chain experts, and marketing and advertising agencies for strategic partnerships. They held workshops to confirm the essence of the brand and isolated Tang's core asset: It tastes better than water, and it is environmentally more sustainable, cheaper, and healthier than carbonated beverages. This led the team to broaden the positioning of Tang by setting it up to compete against water rather than against other powdered beverages. The brand positioning became: "Tang makes water exciting."

"Having a blank check for Tang allowed us to think differently," says Gustavo Abelenda. "Our small, virtually connected team had the freedom to develop a global framework for the brand, quickly scale up local innovations, and use global technology to drive explosive growth."

CADBURY INDIA'S SWEET SUCCESS

When Kraft Foods acquired Cadbury in February 2010, India became one of the ten priority markets for Kraft. Cadbury had taken more than forty years to grow the business to $400 million by 2009, but Kraft recognized that the brand had the Three Ms and the India team was strong.

During one of Kraft leadership's first visits in February 2010, Kraft offered a blank check to the Indian team to make Cadbury in India a half-billion-dollar business by the end of the year—which meant accelerating the region's growth plans and increasing total sales by 25 percent.

"We turned around the proposal in just a few short days," recalls Anand Kripalu, then president of Kraft South Asia and Indochina. "It was quickly approved, and the next day we shared our new $500 million target with our employees. At first, people thought we had lost our minds. But that fear turned to inspiration, once employees realized that we'd been given the freedom and resources to take our business to a new level."

The Cadbury India blank-check team decided to focus on Cadbury Dairy Milk, a chocolate bar that represents the company's biggest brand in India. Just as the Tang team had decided to focus on Tang Orange, the Cadbury team saw that Dairy Milk had the Three Ms: momentum, attractive margins, and, as the most important part of Cadbury's Indian business, Dairy Milk was material.

The initial blank-check proposal called for expanding

distribution, increasing the marketing spend, and investing in sales. When the team evaluated distribution channels, for example, team members observed that in some retail outlets, Cadbury Dairy Milk was stored and displayed in "visi coolers"—enclosed cases that give Cadbury visibility at the retail location and keep the chocolate from melting in India's fierce summer heat. The outlets that had visi coolers beat sales at comparable outlets by 15 percent. On the principle of leveraging what works, the proposal called for doubling the number of locations with visi coolers from 20,000 to 40,000. The team also planned to double permanent in-store displays for Cadbury Dairy Milk from 5,000 to 10,000 and expand distribution into 2,100 additional towns and villages—bringing the total number of sales outlets to 550,000 in India. Finally, they planned to increase investment in Cadbury Dairy Milk advertising and promotions by 45 percent.

Also echoing the Tang experience, the blank-check process drove the Cadbury team to reconsider the core asset, which eventually led to the expansion of the franchise beyond chocolate into a larger market of sweets.

We will save details of the execution for later, but suffice it to say that the results were transformational. In 2010, Cadbury India had its best year ever, with almost 28 percent revenue growth—doubling its original growth targets and exceeding the $500 million blank-check target. The best part? The team did not spend all the money it had asked for and returned a significant portion of the blank-check allocation.

BREAKING THE MOLD IN CHINA

The blank-check approach can operate beyond brands and transform an entire business. We've already talked about the problems faced a decade ago by Kraft China. Despite years of huge investments, by 2007 Kraft China's business was still small by Kraft's standards, less than $150 million in annual revenues. And worse, it was plagued by low gross margins; growth for the sake of growth was a waste of time because there was no hope of making money. There seemed to be no point in scaling up something that was not working.

Still, China had been chosen as one of the 5-10-10 markets because Kraft leadership continued to believe in its potential. The company had developed an infrastructure there—a sales force, distribution machinery, and so on—that could be the basis for a turnaround. But the model was off. It was time to take the way the company did business in China and flip it on its head—and a blank-check initiative was the catalyst for that change.

"We knew that Lorna Davis, who was China's new business leader, and Shawn Warren from our regional office, who knew our categories and brands well, would make the perfect pair to lead this transformational initiative," recalls Pradeep Pant, president of Kraft Asia Pacific. "Both had the drive, the creativity, and an inspiring leadership style to make it happen."

Davis and Warren rose to the challenge laid down by Kraft's leadership. In eight weeks in 2008, the Davis-Warren blank-check team came back with a proposal that defied conventional logic: Scale back the business they were trying to expand.

Their proposal aligned squarely with the company's 5-10-10 strategy. The blank-check team decided to focus the portfolio on a few things that had the best shots at turning into big winners. At the time, Kraft had recently bought Danone's Chinese business, and the two companies together had scores of brands. "Trying to do too many things all subscale is just a nightmare in a country as complicated as China," says Davis, who headed Danone in China before its purchase by Kraft. Given the 5-10-10 framework, the team knew its focus categories (such as biscuits/cookies) and brands (such as Oreo). But the necessary distorting of resources led to some tough confrontations. "There's that moment when you actually have to say, 'I'm not going to put money on this,'" Davis recalls. "And you've got a brand manager crying in your office and a marketing director telling you that the world will end if you don't advertise this or that."

The China team also proposed to invest in deepening their local talent pool so they could get closer to Chinese consumers. That would start with offering competitive salaries, but the team also had two other prime inducements. New hires could be promised extraordinary freedom to operate, and they would be offered significant time for community activities. Davis and Warren wanted to boost the local talent to leverage a "glocal" approach that combined the best of global technology and expertise with local market know-how (see chapter 8). "Having the freedom of a blank check helped us take risks, think bigger, and look at the business with fresh eyes," recalls Warren.

DEALING WITH FAILURES

Blank checks produce spectacular results when they work. As with all innovation efforts, however, a certain percentage will fail. Business leaders need to be prepared for initiatives that fall short. There are two important lessons in dealing with failures—learn from them and overcome the fear of failure.

Not long ago, Kraft dealt with a blank-check disappointment in Latin America, where the company thought it saw a large opportunity to drive growth by developing nutritious yet affordable products for low-income consumers. A Latin American team took on a blank-check challenge and came up with an affordable, nutritious dessert under the Royal brand—a line of gelatins and puddings fortified with vitamins and containing 45 percent less sugar. The desserts tasted good and the price points were affordable. The team also managed to build awareness and secure good distribution. But the products failed to sell well, and the gross margins were lower than expected. The initiative was quickly canceled.

The Kraft leaders and the blank-check team took away several important lessons from this failure. The product involved changing consumers' attitudes and behavior—a difficult and lengthy process. The positioning of the product as a "treat" did not resonate with target consumers. And the business model turned out to be unsustainable: Costs were too high, and the company could not price the desserts appropriately while still earning an acceptable gross margin.

Here's what's probably the most important point: The team

leading the initiative was not penalized. They had shown imagination and energy, and afterward they could articulate what had gone wrong. Despite the failure, the team leader was promoted to head the snacks business in Brazil.

TIPS FOR MANAGING BLANK CHECKS

Through our experience with blank-check initiatives in different product categories and markets, we have identified some important principles for improving the odds of success.

Focus on what matters. Blank checks must always aim at what matters to the business. At Kraft, blank checks were always linked to the company's focus strategy.

Create sustainable growth. Blank checks can produce phenomenal revenue growth, but this growth should be both profitable and sustainable over time. Business leaders should be careful that teams don't undertake initiatives that can boost revenues in the short term but will hurt the business in the longer term. The test-and-learn approach is critical. Start small, measure milestones, prove the success, then build fast. Even in China, the initial blank check was small.

Innovate broadly. To harness the full potential of their businesses, teams need to take a broad view of innovation that goes well beyond creating new products. They need to innovate with packaging, promotions, advertising, distribution, and partnerships.

Simplify everything. Blank checks should be the enemy of the complexity that often strangles companies. Blank checks should strive for simplification. This can be achieved in the product (for example, by reducing performance or features to "just enough" levels desired by consumers); in the process (manufacturing, distribution, sales); in the organization (removing layers and moving decision making closer to local markets); and in administration (faster decision making and fewer meetings).

Kraft leadership gave the company's supply chain people in Central and Eastern Europe a blank check to raise productivity by 50 percent in twelve months—a hefty boost under any circumstances. The blank-check team realized they had to approach the business in a fresh way. They brought in experts from outside, simplified processes, and cut the number of items on the price list, focusing on those that mattered. They beat their target in less than nine months.

Don't overdo it. It is easy to get carried away by the success of blank checks and approve too many. Blank checks are powerful tools, but they are very demanding in terms of both financial resources and leadership bandwidth. They will produce revenue and profit increases in the long run, but they require significant investments in the short term. They also require a lot of personal attention from business leaders. Just as venture capitalists limit the number of start-up investments they make and the number of company boards they serve on, business leaders need to limit the number of blank checks they administer simultaneously.

Create a family spirit. Blank-check initiatives require every team member to put the collective good of the team above his or her ego and personal point of view. This is the family approach that we have discussed. Incentives should be balanced to recognize individual success, but also the success of the team as a whole. It also helps to host "family dinners" before every major leadership team meeting. Each dinner has a clear agenda focused on two or three business issues that need input from the family. At the end of the dinner, the team arrives at a consensus. This practice gives the team clarity on what needs to be done and promotes a sense of shared ownership of the outcomes.

Spread the word. Blank checks not only serve as powerful engines of growth; they can also have a potent ripple effect. The simple introduction of the concept with its promise of liberation from the usual constraints can serve as an energizer up and down the ranks. The message: This company is changing. That in itself can generate more new thinking, more fresh ideas. And the blank-check projects can't help but channel attention as people follow (and, one hopes, cheer on) the success of the new ventures. Therefore, news of the blank checks should be circulated, the successes celebrated, and even the lessons of failure should be passed along. Everyone in the company should benefit from the experience.

As discussed above, blank checks—for all their potential impact—are just one tool in the Focus7 arsenal. They need to be used selectively and only when they fit with the overall strategy. And just as every blank check—regardless of the inspiration contained in its originating proposal—requires careful execution, so does every element in the Focus7 framework. How to execute is the subject of the next chapter.

STEP 4—PEOPLE:

UNLEASH POTENTIAL

1. To drive disproportionate growth, place big and bold bets on a few key people to lead the growth initiatives.
2. In choosing leaders of the initiatives, look for people who have passion and energy, who understand the value of working on a team, and who are driven to improve and to innovate.
3. Distort resources to support growth initiatives—concentrating money, people, skills, and effort behind the priorities, while taking resources from nonpriority areas.
4. In extraordinary cases, distorting resources can take the form of a blank check—an offer to a select team of

almost unlimited resources to meet extraordinary targets within a defined time frame.

5. Blank checks are a way to offer freedom within a framework—while the team has broad authority on resources and implementation, every blank-check initiative must fit within the strategic framework and must satisfy the Three *M*s: Momentum, Margin, and Materiality.

CHAPTER 7

EXECUTION:
SIMPLIFY AND DELEGATE

Thinking, talking, and planning are all fine and necessary. But following up, turning ideas into action, comes as the real test. In our Focus7 journey so far, we have discussed placing your bets, getting the word out, and empowering people. With these elements in place, the next step is to make things happen. Execution stands as the less sexy but far more important handmaiden of strategy. Again, Focus7 relies on simple principles—*Stop* doing things that are not aligned with priorities. *Simplify* your organization and your processes. *Delegate* to allow people to make better decisions. *Accelerate* your decision making by starting small, testing and learning, and then when justified scaling fast.

To see how these themes of execution played out at Kraft, let's return to Kraft China in 2007. When Kraft Foods bought the cookie and cracker division of the French company Danone in late 2007, Kraft acquired a portfolio of famous brands, such as the Petit Déjeuner, one of Europe's most popular treats. And it also acquired Lorna Davis, a lively South African veteran of the food industry who oversaw the Danone biscuit business in China. With the acquisition, she took over Kraft China.

At the time, Kraft and Danone ran very different operations. "Kraft had a much more ambitious vision for China than Danone did," Davis recalls. "So, for example, Kraft wanted to be in all of the big centers. They wanted to build really strong relationships with all the big retailers, which drove a very, very high cost base. Danone was a much more pay-as-you-go sort of culture. In fact, I think Danone was undercapitalized and underdeveloped for the future. Kraft, though, was at the other end of the spectrum."

Davis's first job was to integrate the two businesses. Meantime, Kraft's new international leadership introduced Davis to the transformative mantra of less is more—focus. "Both companies had too many brands," Davis says. "When you put them together, the problem was twice as bad." Her come-to-Jesus moment, as she puts it, arrived a few months after joining the business. "Everyone gets the focus idea—that these five things matter more than those twenty-five things, but it's really the moment when you actively agree to stop doing stuff that it hits home. Delete a brand. Stop advertising. Remove a brand manager. People changes, money changes. That's when it really is painful. Until you really crack the resource allocation, you can have as much rhetoric as you like, it doesn't sink in. That was when it sank in."

Davis was coming face-to-face with execution—the most important step in Focus7 and also the most difficult. You can have the best strategy in the world, a blueprint laid out with exquisite vision and precise detail. The strategy can come with a tested track record from the best consultants money can buy. But talk is cheap—execution usually makes the difference between success and failure. To put it more starkly: Success is 90 percent execution, 10 percent everything else.

Like many of the elements of Focus7, the four principles of execution may seem obvious, but like so much in business (and life) they get easily overwhelmed or lost in the hurly-burly of the moment.

STOP DOING STUFF

We've said it before, but it's such a key element of Focus7 that it bears repeating: To get focused you need to stop doing things that take too much effort to achieve very little. You and your business can't take on everything at once. As we have emphasized in talking about distorting resources, you have to concentrate on areas of the business that have real potential, while cutting back or eliminating products or ventures that are just getting by—exactly what Lorna Davis and Kraft China did in deciding to stop spreading efforts among more than twenty brands and instead give priority to a handful. In a similar way, one of the Tang team's first actions was to halt many of the small initiatives and divert resources to the core product, Tang Orange.

Stopping things is almost never simple. Every brand, product, or initiative has a devoted constituency, so for a leader it often takes fortitude to make the hard decisions. That kind of discipline lives at the heart of successful execution, however. Steve Jobs knew this. "There is no one better at turning off the noise that is going on around him," Apple's Tim Cook told Walter Isaacson, Jobs's biographer. "That allows him to focus on a few things and say no to many things. Few people are really good at that."

The noise Cook mentions can come from all directions. In many large organizations, activity gets confused with output. People stay busy, often with work that's internally focused, feeding the beast of corporate processes. Endless time gets wasted preparing tedious reports that get sucked into a relentless cycle of self-regard—think of it as internal combustion that produces no forward motion.

Even start-up companies can get caught up in doing too much stuff. Mohan saw this recently while conferring with the founder of VMock, a start-up Mohan has been advising since its infancy. Salil Pande is an enthusiastic entrepreneur who had created a number of innovative services to marry social media with recruiting. One, VMock Screen, allows companies to conduct virtual video interviews with job candidates. Another, VMock Prep, allows job candidates to practice their interview technique by uploading short videos and getting feedback from peers. The service called VMock Instant Résumé lets candidates submit their résumés online and get instant automated feedback. Pande had several more products in the pipeline, and new ideas kept surfacing. The result—the company had bogged down. Pande's limited development team was overextended trying to move ahead on so many fronts, and the sales effort was flagging because the team was trying to do different types of deals with a range of potential clients, from corporations to schools to individuals.

At a strategy meeting in the fall of 2013, Mohan asked Pande what he thought was VMock's highest-potential initiative. "The Instant Résumé," Pande responded. "People love the fact that they can upload their résumé, get a score that is based on benchmarking against millions of résumés in VMock's database, and get concrete recommendations for improvement."

Mohan pressed: "So why are you doing all this other stuff? Drop all these projects and focus on the one initiative that will make a difference."

At first, Pande hesitated—his team had invested huge efforts and emotions in the other products. On reflection, though, he saw the need to kill them and concentrate on the Instant Résumé. The result: The team is focused, the product is coming along faster, and the message is simpler. This is the first lesson of execution—stop doing stuff that distracts you from what really needs to get done.

SIMPLIFY EVERYTHING

As companies grow, they accumulate bureaucratic procedures and processes that gum up the works. Ask yourself a few questions about how your company makes decisions. How many layers does a report go through in working its way from the front lines to the boss? Should it really take that many people to sign off on an action? Does every procedure have a reason to exist? Is busywork keeping people occupied but adding questionable value? Are too many people attending meetings? And are there too many meetings?

Mohan recalls a conversation with Glenn Lurie, the president of Emerging Enterprises and Partnerships at AT&T. Lurie talked about how he avoided business as usual when he was leading the venture that eventually became AT&T Digital Life, a security and automation offering for homes that AT&T launched in the spring of 2013. When AT&T sought to acquire Xanboo, a start-up that could help build the Digital Life platform, the team from the start-up worried about how quickly AT&T could move. They asked a number of questions: Who would decide? What would the decision process look like? Who would they need to talk to and negotiate with? The Xanboo team was taken aback by Lurie's response—"You only need to deal with me." And the deal got done at lightning speed.

Operating through business as usual, most large companies take forever to make decisions because so many layers of hierarchy are involved. If you want to move fast, cut, de-layer, and simplify.

Simplification extends to meetings. Consider the last few business meetings you have sat through at your company and ask three questions. First, did everyone absolutely need to be there? Second, did you waste time just sharing information that people could have read on their own? Third, how much time was spent in analyzing what happened versus deciding what to do now (*Karna Kya Hai?*)? In a recent meeting of a company where Mohan serves on the board, he and his fellow board members drew the line when their meeting binder bloated to six hundred pages of detailed PowerPoint slides. These beautiful slides had been assembled by dozens of executives toiling hundreds of hours. But the presentation overlooked two simple questions: What was the purpose of all that data? And what was the board being asked to do? The management team realized that most of the presentation dealt with *reporting* on what was happening rather than teeing up the strategic questions for the board's input. The company has since radically simplified its presentations to the board. Further, every presentation has a cover page that summarizes the objective and the decisions or advice being sought. Meetings are shorter, discussions more productive, and the board is now better positioned to provide counsel.

Keep in mind: When you are simplifying and de-layering, you are effectively redirecting energy to endeavors that really count.

DELEGATE AUTHORITY

For the last few decades, the traditional role of leadership has been changing. The old view that leaders are visionaries who have the answers is giving way to a more enlightened approach, one that treats leaders as facilitators who inspire their people to find the answers. The change is well documented. Books have been written, consultancies organized, transformations undertaken.

Leadership's role is changing for a reason. In part, the change reflects a modern world that is generally moving away from a dependence on hierarchy, a process that has accelerated with the rise of the Internet. In a business context, the logic is determinedly practical—you simply get a better outcome by moving decision making and accountability closer to customers and consumers and giving the people responsible for results the operating freedom they need. The approach amounts to looking out the window instead of looking in the mirror. Getting an external view of the world.

But old attitudes die as hard as old habits, and too many organizations continue to operate on the assumption that the bosses back at headquarters enjoy superior knowledge on almost any subject. This belief has any number of unfortunate side effects, from discouraging initiative to encouraging managers to assume that success lies in pleasing the executives above them rather than winning in the marketplace.

Ten or so years ago Kraft Foods had become such a complex matrix that accountability had become fragmented across functions, markets, and business units. Compounding the problem, decision making had become highly centralized. Corporate headquarters in Northfield, Illinois, decided such matters as product pricing, a process that stretched time and excluded the rich knowledge and context of local markets. Even such routine decisions as the pricing of coffee in Germany were being made in a Chicago suburb.

When Irene Rosenfeld arrived in 2006 and Sanjay joined soon after, the role of headquarters became more strategic and less operational. Certain decisions, such as those involving food safety, IT, and purchasing, remained centralized because they had to be made on a large scale. But the decisions that demanded intimacy with the local marketplace were delegated, and the change had a profound effect in making the organization more nimble.

That new agility paid off in countless ways, but here's a small example that reflects the new world of communications: In 2013 the Super Bowl, the championship extravaganza of American professional football, was held in the Mercedes-Benz Superdome, a huge indoor arena in New Orleans. Kraft arranged for several members of Oreo's American marketing team to be sitting by in New York with digital experts in front of a TV screen to provide tweets during the game. Just after the second half started, the Superdome suffered a power outage—the place went black and the game stopped. Back in New York, the digital team got to work and quickly cobbled up a tweet playing off Oreo's venerable "Twist, Lick, Dunk" campaign. The Oreo marketers approved, and the tweet went out within minutes: "Power out? No problem. You can still dunk in the dark." *Ad Age* reported that the makeshift ad was retweeted ten thousand times in the next hour, and in the postmortems on the game's advertising portfolio, the Oreo tweet was widely acclaimed a coup. Daniel Terdiman of CNET called it "so brilliant and bold that it out and out won the night."

The triumph only came about because the authority to approve the tweet had been pushed down far enough that the decision could be made almost instantaneously.

How do you persuade an organization that the role of leadership has changed? How do you alter ingrained attitudes? There's no simple formula. After all, for most people, the default position is either to defer to higher-ups or to fall into the cover-your-ass syndrome. You've got to say it and say it again and again and even then assume that most people won't believe you. So you've got to follow up with actions—assign P&L responsibility; tell the manager who calls for your approval that the decision is his or hers; above all, don't second-guess. That means sitting through plenty of mistakes made by the newly empowered—just make sure the people responsible have learned something.

The notorious Vegemite uproar provides a good case in point. Australians cherish their Vegemite—a dark brown food paste made from yeast extract and various vegetable and spice additives. It is a popular spread for sandwiches and toast, and has an ardent following in Australia. Kraft, which owns the brand, wanted to introduce a new variety—Vegemite mixed with cream cheese—but needed a name, and Kraft Australia decided to call the new product Vegemite iSnack 2.0. Australians immediately erupted in disdain, going on the Internet to deride the name as dumb, forgettable, and—worst of all—un-Australian.

All this unfolded outside the knowledge of Kraft corporate headquarters—authority had been delegated to Kraft Australia and all decisions were made there. Sanjay first learned of the commotion when George Zoghbi, head of Kraft Australia at that time, called to warn him that a story was coming in *The Wall Street Journal.* The authority for solving the problem stayed with Kraft Australia, too. Within four days, the company announced it would shelve iSnack 2.0 and put the choice of a new name up to a vote by consumers. The winner came back—Cheesybite—and the controversy disappeared quickly.

As we will discuss more fully in a later chapter, even with the delegation of authority, leaders of big companies still need to strike a balance between local and global. While the managers closest to the marketplace should have the authority to make key decisions, the mother company's resources—in expertise, technology, R&D, procurement—should be made available across the board. That's where the headquarters leadership can bear down—making sure the folks on the front lines have the tools they need.

The key here is clarifying roles—wringing any ambiguity out of who does what where—and then rigorously holding to the arrangement. If a local operation resists, say, adopting a company-wide IT system, corporate leadership needs to stay tough and insist. In the case of Kraft China, the company had made it absolutely clear to Lorna Davis that she was in charge of the P&L, so once the turmoil of integration had settled, she couldn't sit back and wait for her bosses to tell her what to do next—she had to get down to running the business.

Once the roles have been clarified and the authority pushed down close to the customer, the corporate leadership should step aside, help with resources, and, of course, monitor progress. The lower-tier managers should run the business on their own and inform the bosses when key decisions have been made or significant developments have unfolded. What's the standard for alerting higher-ups? One classic shibboleth: If something could land in *The Wall Street Journal*, tell the boss first. No executive wants to learn from a news account about a decision made by a unit that reports to him.

ACCELERATE ACTION BY STARTING SMALL, TESTING AND LEARNING, SCALING FAST

Strategy involves thinking big. But at some point, you have to descend from big-picture thinking to the tactical details of starting *something* quickly. Smart execution involves starting small and testing the initiatives, learning what works and what doesn't, then scaling fast when you've got a business model that works. The bias is for action, but action grounded in knowledge. The point is to get moving and be agile. Get it mostly right and adjust as you go along. You're looking for evidence that a particular initiative can produce continuing, sustainable growth. Apply short timetables—quarterly or every six months.

When an initiative seems to be working, channel more resources in that direction. If something fails or slows down, reduce the allocation. Make constant adjustments.

Companies often stumble in execution when they start big and fail big. We recently saw a vivid demonstration of this at venerable JC Penney. A mid-tier retailer known for its discounts and functional stores, JC Penney hired Ron Johnson from Apple to reignite the business. Johnson brought strong credentials—he'd played a major role at Target, and at Apple he helped pioneer the wonderfully free-flowing and successful Apple stores.

Johnson had a plan to revive JC Penney by knocking out the sales and discounts and upgrading the fashion. But he apparently felt pressed for time, so rather than testing his concepts in small doses and learning as he went, he essentially tossed out the old JC Penney wholesale and brought in the new, imposing his program company-wide. Customers rebelled. Revenues dropped. The stock price sank. And Ron Johnson was out less than a year and a half after he came on board.

With a bias for action, execution is never finished. It's not like tobogganing, where you get a push at the top of the hill and then keep picking up speed through the grace of gravity while you sit tight for a fun ride. On the contrary, execution is a constant process of giving pushes, applying brakes, making turns, always adjusting to maximize results. And once something achieves success—it's hitting sustained profitable growth—the task is to drive execution with boring consistency, repeating the model that works, while constantly seeking improvements.

Let's take a look at how the principles of execution played out in the Tang and Kraft China cases we discussed in the last chapter.

TANG BUILDS ON MOMENTUM

The Tang team scored a success almost immediately by stopping stuff, focusing on Tang Orange and eliminating a lot of small-bore ventures. That cleared space, so to speak, to adopt several innovations, in particular new packaging and a marketing push built around kids, health, and sustainability. The issue then became how to sustain growth—keep the momentum going. And success depended heavily on clarifying roles and delegating authority.

The Tang team started with a consumer insight: Tang could broaden its appeal if it was positioned as a complement to water—"Tang makes water exciting." This positioning highlighted Tang's point of difference against other drinks. Armed with this insight, the team decided to expand the market for the venerable powdered drink by developing new, locally relevant flavors. To do that, Tang needed to draw on Kraft's global technology resources, its expertise in producing powdered beverages. To determine the new flavors, however, the local managers held sway, drawing on local market research to find the flavors to test. In other words, the people closest to the consumer decided what would play locally, and Kraft's engineers produced the powder. This may sound like an obvious outcome, but in fact it required a shift in corporate mindset.

In the end, the flavors chosen reflected the places where the Tang would be drunk—for Mexico, tamarind and *horchata* (a traditional drink flavored with lime and cinnamon). Likewise, the Philippines got mango Tang; Brazil got passion fruit and soursop (a local fruit); and the Middle East got pineapple and lemon mint. And all of these flavors were tested in small markets before they were rolled out. Would they improve profit margins or simply be a distraction? "The fact is that you can come up with the most creative, innovative products, but if they don't connect with consumers, then they don't really matter," says Gustavo Abelenda, president of Kraft Latin America. "And you can never really know until you test them."

The Tang team took the same approach of starting small and scaling fast with other initiatives. For instance, the new Boato sachets for single servings of Tang proved a hit in Brazil. This packaging innovation was then expanded to more than two dozen lines around the world.

For the Tang team, delegating extended beyond the company to its partners. Kraft's main advertising agency was Ogilvy & Mather. Kraft told Ogilvy to put the agency's best talent—wherever it was—to work directly with the Tang team in Brazil. Kraft's leadership was kept informed on what was unfolding in Brazil, but their input wasn't sought and their approval wasn't required. Ogilvy ended up producing a series of lively commercials that have since been expanded to other markets, including Argentina and Mexico.

Although Tang's original orange flavor continues to top the sales charts worldwide, the new local flavors have come to make up about 25 percent of Tang sales in developing markets and have helped immeasurably in expanding the brand.

OREO SCORES IN CHINA

Probably nothing encapsulates successful execution better than the Oreo experience in China. Mark Clouse, who headed Kraft China before Lorna Davis, calls Oreo the "trigger point to get the other pieces done," so it's worth digging deeper into how Oreo helped set off Kraft's Chinese surge.

Kraft had introduced the iconic American cookie to China in 1996, and sales poked along at a reasonable rate, but it was far from a hit, capturing less than 4 percent of the market. "We were selling an American brand and American business to Chinese people," Clouse explains.

Kraft's R&D operation had actually come up with some possible enhancements for the Chinese market. For example, almost by accident—more on that later—researchers had produced a version of the cookie that was slightly less sweet and might connect with the Chinese consumer, who doesn't have the sweet tooth of the typical American. Clouse and his colleagues also came up with a plan to offer Oreos in smaller packages to produce a lower price point. "Initially, I think the belief was that this is a premium product," Clouse says.

But the plans never got the approvals needed from higher-ups. Things got so bad that the word finally came down from headquarters: Take Oreo off the market in China; it's not working.

All that changed when Oreo was named one of the ten priority brands, and Kraft's leadership pushed the decision-making authority down the ladder. Suddenly Clouse—and later Lorna Davis, working with Shawn Warren—had the authority to decide how to run Kraft's Chinese business from the front lines. Given that freedom, the China team recognized the need to change the product and the price to fit the lives of more consumers.

That led to the introduction of a cookie package with a more alluring price point. By offering Oreos in smaller packages (seven cookies instead of fourteen), the company was able to penetrate a far larger proportion of the Chinese population, which was growing more affluent. "The Chinese consumer saw global-brand purchases as part of their own personal journey of growth and prosperity," Clouse says.

The China team also introduced the less sweet Oreo. The backstory to that success turns out to be a bit convoluted, however—and also teaches something about successful execution. "The R&D people tell me that they were actually kind of embarrassed about the formula in China because they were trying to match the U.S. exactly, but the flour was different," says Lorna Davis. "Everything's a little bit different [in China], and they sort of ended up slightly less sweet—and thank goodness for that."

In other words, dialing back the sweetness of the Oreo in China was partly a function of luck. "I had this boss in England who used to tell me that whenever something happens, people think that it's either a conspiracy or a cock-up," Davis adds with a laugh. "People love to believe conspiracy because it's more elaborate, but the reality is that most of the mistakes or most of the things that happen in life are cock-ups. The longer I'm in business, the more I realize that there are lots of things that are simply luck."

She's right—but it was only with the local focus and the willingness to test that Kraft could capitalize on the new flavor. In other words, it took careful execution to take advantage of the luck.

The Kraft China team continued to produce a stream of Oreo innovations. The cream filling in the Chinese cookie now comes in a variety of local flavors, including strawberry and green tea. And the marketing effort has both expanded and changed. The China team wanted to hire Yao Ming, the former NBA star, for a series of lively commercials. Who decides? After all, it's a global brand, and the famous face appearing in a commercial can affect the brand's reputation. Kraft China decided. The higher-ups in Northfield were simply informed.

The decision paid off, as the new commercials caught the growing wave of Chinese response to emotional (as opposed to rational) advertising. "I think we tapped into a vein that was very powerful because for Chinese people, with the one-child family, it's a huge deal to connect with their kids," Davis says, "and Oreo gave them that language. I remember being shocked, struck by how Chinese consumers really connected to the twist, lick, dunk thing and the idea of sitting across from your kid and sharing an Oreo. It really just touched their hearts in a way I had never seen advertising do before."

Oreo became the number-one cookie in China, with a 13 percent market share, a success that saw Oreo revenues in developing markets grow from less than $200 million in 2006 to $1 billion in 2012.

When Oreo started responding well with stimuli such as blank checks, the priority turned to figuring out how to make Oreo even bigger. The brand was driving a Virtuous Cycle of Growth (see chapter 11), growth that was sustaining itself. The brand was growing faster than the market, with above-average gross margins. What's more, the brand had a phenomenal emotional connection with local consumers—it had soul—making it less vulnerable to volatile economic conditions and changes in raw material prices.

The teams responsible for Tang and Oreo worked both globally and locally to ensure that the big, bold bets they'd made on the brands paid off. In the next chapter, we will take a closer look at the organizational structures that can help make successes like that possible.

WHAT TO DO IF YOUR WORLD CHANGES

What do you do if the market gets disrupted? Or your core business suddenly faces a mortal threat? You can't put your head in the sand and hope the trouble will disappear—simply continuing to focus on what worked in the past won't pull you through. The business world is full of sad stories of companies operating in a market that changed quickly and dramatically— Nokia and Kodak, for example.

And that's exactly what happened about three decades ago in India to Unilever with its core business of detergents.

At the time, the Anglo-Dutch conglomerate had a successful brand called Surf, which was at the top end of the market, providing the whitest wash. But Surf was winning in a relatively small patch, the high-end demographic. In fact, powdered detergents in general were premium products in India, because the vast majority of the population couldn't afford them. In rural areas, many people still washed clothes in rivers and streams using unbranded laundry soap.

Then an enterprising Indian chemist, Karsanbhai Patel, came up with a formula for a cheap detergent, Nirma—named after his daughter—that aimed for the so-called bottom of the demographic pyramid. Nirma provided consumers with acceptable cleaning at less than one-third the price of Surf. Aided by an aggressive marketing campaign anchored by a catchy jingle, Nirma grew from a small, regional brand to an Indian powerhouse. By 1985 Nirma was on its way to becoming one of the largest detergent brands by volume in the world.

What should Unilever do? When Surf came under pressure and Nirma was growing fast, Sanjay had just returned from the United Kingdom to India as Hindustan Unilever (HUL) India's marketing manager for detergents. The first task was to look to the core and try to grow Surf and improve its profitability. HUL researchers improved Surf's quality. The company raised the detergent's price. Then HUL relaunched the detergent with a celebrated ad campaign featuring a no-nonsense woman named Lalitaji, who became the personification of the value provided by Surf. The brand started growing and profitability improved.

That still left the matter of Nirma. HUL faced several choices. On the one hand, it could just ignore the new rival. After all, Nirma might be opening a new market, but it wasn't HUL's traditional market. Presumably, Nirma's low-end customers would move up to Surf as they became more sophisticated and climbed the economic ladder. In any case, Hindustan Unilever wasn't equipped to compete at Nirma's price—and what was the point, since the margins were so low?

On the other hand, Nirma showed signs of becoming a genuine threat. As the brand established itself, Nirma was likely to try to compete with HUL in the premium markets. And Nirma customers were more likely to stay with a brand they knew. If HUL didn't do something now, it could get murdered in the future. Besides, why should Hindustan Unilever be content to compete in the small, high-end market when the entire consumer market was far bigger and growing?

In the end, Sanjay and his colleagues decided to take on Nirma directly, but did it by starting quietly, almost surreptitiously. They recognized that the key to success was not to imitate Nirma, but to improve on it, while keeping at or close to Nirma's price point. And they knew that in facing a disrupted market, the best bet was to build on an existing strength of giant Unilever. In this case, that was the company's expertise and technological advantage in creating powdered detergents. Sanjay and his colleagues operated on a key principle: A low price for the product didn't necessarily mean it had to be of low quality.

A small, local, multifunctional team devised a plan called STING—Strategy to Inhibit Nirma's Growth. Unilever's international stable of scientists created a low-cost detergent that improved on Nirma by almost every measure, particularly on kindness to hands and clothes. The marketing and distribution of this new product were managed locally.

The Indian team named the detergent Wheel and tested it in small runs. When the product showed signs of selling well, distribution expanded. Wheel's marketing took on Nirma directly with a hip and provocative campaign, designed and produced locally. Wheel caught on immediately and soon was challenging Nirma in the low-end market. Today, Wheel has become hugely successful and one of HUL's largest brands.

The Wheel success story grew from a moment that was almost desperate and called for a dramatic and rapid response. The solution lay in coming up with a significantly new business model. Wheel differed from Surf in almost all aspects—price, production costs, distribution, and marketing. The revenue model went from high price/low volume to low price/high volume.

Early on, because Wheel was managed so differently from the rest of the HUL businesses—far more lean and mean—the question became whether to integrate Wheel into the regular operation or run it as a separate unit. The concern was that if Wheel became part of the regular operation with the attendant costs, HUL wouldn't be able to make money on it. Sanjay and his colleagues ultimately recommended that it be run separately, but with linkage to the mother ship in areas that would leverage HUL's scope and muscle, such as technology and

R&D. The point was to maintain the lower costs of a new, small company while taking advantage of the strengths of the larger, established enterprise.

Was taking on Nirma worth it? Wheel's margins are lower than Surf's, though revenue is far larger. More important, Wheel challenged Nirma's expansion, and thirty years later, Unilever remains the category leader in India.

The case offers several lessons:

- While you to have to focus where you can win, if there is a market disruption, you have to redefine your focus. But that doesn't mean abandoning your core—rather it means building on your strengths to adjust to the new normal. If that requires offering a new product, creating a new distribution system, implementing a new production process—whatever—the key is to start small, test, learn, and scale up quickly when the results look promising.
- Learn from your competitors. HUL didn't copy Nirma, but the company learned from Nirma's experience and then drew on Unilever's strength to compete on Nirma's level.
- The biggest threat to any organization is complacency. As a leader, it's important to encourage internal disrupters, to create a low-grade sense of impatience that can be tapped to fuel constant experimentation and testing.
- Ideally, you are in a continuous process of creating new markets by providing consumers with products, services, and experiences they don't know they need.

STEP 5—EXECUTION:

SIMPLIFY AND DELEGATE

1. Strategy is useless without execution—the real test of a leader comes with turning ideas into action. Execution gets bogged down when companies try to do too much and when too much decision making comes from the top and goes through too many layers.

2. To speed up execution, stop doing marginal stuff—trim or eliminate initiatives that aren't making substantial contributions and are sapping energy from executing on what really matters.

3. Simplify by cutting bureaucracy, eliminating layers in decision making, and increasing the speed of information flow across the organization.
4. Delegate authority by moving decision making and accountability closer to customers and giving the people responsible for results the operating freedom they need.
5. Start small but scale fast. Get it mostly right, test, learn, and adjust as you go along. Once the model works, execute with boring consistency, seeking continuous improvement.

CHAPTER 8

ORGANIZATION:
ALIGN AND COLLABORATE

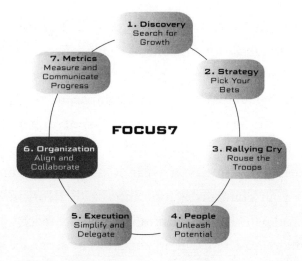

We have talked about matching skills and talent with strategic initiatives, delegating authority, and excelling in execution. But people don't exist in a vacuum in a company. They are part of an organization. They belong to a business unit, a function, or a department—the typical dimensions around which organizations are structured. For the most part, the point is to conduct business as usual efficiently. Often, however, growth is not about conducting business as usual. Growth requires seizing opportunities.

This chapter addresses how to align your organization around opportunities. This is the next step in Focus7—creating the opportunity-driven organization. Doing so requires agility and leverages the forces of globalization and digitalization to achieve competitive advantage. The chapter also discusses how you get the balance right between being hopelessly local and mindlessly global.

First, though, a word of caution: If it ain't broke, don't fix it. Don't reorganize for the sake of change. Avoid radical surgery except when absolutely necessary. And don't make reorganizations a habitual event, like a hurricane that blows in year after year. Sales are flat and profits are down? Reorganize! Competition is stealing market share? Reorganize! A new leadership team has arrived? Reorganize! A consulting firm says your company is too centralized? Reorganize! Oh, now the company is too decentralized! Reorganize!

Too many leaders use reorganization as a panacea for all ills. Or they hope the flurry of activity will signal that they are serious about change. While every business has to change from time to time to deal with evolving market conditions and new corporate strategy, reorganization is a tool that should be used with utmost care. Constant reorganization can push folks into a state of perpetual anxiety and internal focus. It saps corporate productivity, increases employee turnover, and leads to a loss of knowledge and relationships that people have built up in their jobs.

Remember: If you want to change your fortunes, sometimes you have to stay put and just execute. Strive to be boringly consistent and relentless about execution. Give your strategy a fair chance to play out.

Of course, sometimes radical reorganization does become a strategic necessity—particularly when there is a dramatic change in technology, markets, or the competitive landscape. Microsoft, a consulting client of Mohan's for more than a decade, faced such a situation. The tech giant has traditionally been a product-driven operation, developing software and platforms across a broad range of applications for consumers and businesses. With iconic products such as Microsoft Office, Windows, Windows Server, and Xbox, the company has enjoyed enormous success. Over a dozen distinct products and services each bring in revenues of more than $1 billion a year.

In recent years, Microsoft's markets have changed substantially. The rise of cloud computing provides software as a service over a network, and the rapid growth of mobile devices threatens Microsoft's traditional business of selling software for personal computers. Customers want services and devices that allow them to work and play however and wherever they want. Microsoft needs to offer things that consumers and businesses can use for their high-value activities.

This disruptive change has spurred Microsoft to announce an ambitious transformation from a "software and platforms" company to a "devices and services" company that will connect its broad offerings into solutions for consumers and businesses. Microsoft's new direction makes sense, but it means the company has to realign its organization with the strategy. The different product groups need to collaborate on creating the services and devices of the future.

After years of operating as a loose confederation of business divisions, Microsoft announced one of the most sweeping reorganizations in the company's history in the summer of 2013. The new structure aims to rally people behind "One Microsoft." Instead of being organized around key products, such as Windows, the company will be arranged according to areas of expertise, such as operating systems and devices. For the first time, all the engineering expertise for a technology will come under one umbrella. For example, the Operating Systems Engineering Group will work on the PC, tablet, smartphone, and TV operating systems to create a more integrated customer experience.

Though sometimes necessary, any radical reorganization is fraught with risk and has to be executed carefully to ensure that the business is not derailed.

OPPORTUNITY-FOCUSED ORGANIZATIONS

Several leading companies today are creating internal groups whose charter is to pursue specific cross-company growth opportunities that would otherwise fall through the cracks of organizational boundaries. This is the idea of focus applied to organizations. You can't get the whole organization to change what it does well, which is to pursue business as usual. But you can create an *opportunity-focused organization*.

IBM, for example, has worked hard to do exactly that. Mike

Giersch, IBM's former vice president of strategy, talked about his experience with the company's Emerging Business Opportunities program at the Kellogg School of Management a few years ago. According to Giersch, IBM recognized that its management system rewarded execution directed at short-term results and did not place enough value on strategic business building. IBM was very good at serving established markets with existing offerings, but it was doing a poor job of building new businesses in nascent markets. It lacked an organized approach to pursue game-changing opportunities. In 2000, IBM started creating so-called Emerging Business Opportunities (EBO) units, directing them to identify and pursue "white space" opportunities that could become profitable, billion-dollar businesses within five to seven years. These individual EBOs are housed in the appropriate business division, but they are given special treatment. Each EBO has an IBM executive "champion," a special support structure, protected funding, and well-defined mechanisms for cross-company alignment. EBOs are also measured differently from traditional businesses—the focus is on achieving strategic milestones and not on hitting revenue targets.

By 2006, IBM had launched twenty-five EBOs, which introduced new businesses such as Blade Servers, Business Process Integration, Flexible Hosting Services, Storage Software, Grid Computing, and Information-Based Medicine. Five of the EBOs had achieved $1 billion or more in revenues. While three of the twenty-five EBOs had failed, the remaining twenty-two produced over 15 percent of IBM's total revenues! Had IBM not created an opportunity-focused organization, it was very unlikely that it would have been able to pursue these white-space opportunities in a fast, focused, and flexible manner.

CREATING COLLABORATIVE NETWORKS

How do you set up an opportunity-focused organization? Collaborative networks—teams that come together from all over around a common goal—represent the modern organizing principle for businesses that want to flourish. It's hard to imagine a major business initiative today that doesn't involve a collaborative network of some sort, even if it arose by happenstance and the only boundaries being broken are those separating the divisions within a company. And there's no magic formula to the creation of a collaborative network.

However, Mohan has devised a blueprint that can serve as a guide for any company seeking to create an opportunity-focused organization. The key is to set up an Innovation Hub to serve as a catalyst for incubating, launching, and scaling innovation initiatives. The Innovation Hub would follow the principles of *Fewer, Bigger, Bolder* by focusing on a small number of carefully selected projects—not more than three to four at a time. This would allow the company to allocate resources behind the projects and give them high visibility. What's more, in setting up an Innovation Hub, it will inevitably take time to iron out the kinks in the operating model, so it would be better to "think big but start small," rather than starting with a large number of initiatives before the model has been refined with experience.

The potential projects for the Innovation Hub should be carefully selected and feature the following characteristics:

1. They have the potential to be game-changers for the company.
2. They require collaboration across lines of business and geographies.
3. They are potentially disruptive to the company's existing businesses.
4. They cannot be brought to life with the business-as-usual mindset and culture.
5. They need to be pursued with a sense of urgency.

The projects would be selected based on input from the company's leadership, with the CEO being the ultimate decision maker to ensure that the selections align with strategy. The project teams would consist of high-potential individuals nominated by the leadership team. Team members would be dedicated to their projects, with a minimum commitment of one year. Each project team would consist of between four and six core members, with a mix of experienced and young executives and at least one external member from outside the company (a consultant or an academic). Ideally, team members would be drawn from several different lines of business and functions, to provide a diversity of perspectives and expertise. Project teams would be self-managed, and each team would be colocated to encourage face-to-face interaction among people drawn from very different parts of the company.

The teams would be provided with seed funding for their projects based on a concise business case (two to three pages maximum) that outlined the initiative, the value proposition for customers, the anticipated benefits for the company, the proposed development and validation approach, a proposed time line, financial resources required, and ninety-day milestones. Further funding would be provided contingent on achievement of milestone commitments. Project progress would be monitored through monthly reports and coaching sessions, as well as through quarterly milestone meetings with the leadership team. A steering committee of top executives and an external expert would provide more regular oversight. The Innovation Hub would aggressively market itself within the company to attract the right talent and to convince prospective team members that being selected for an Innovation Hub team was a badge of honor, and no stigma attaches if the project fails.

Here's a key point: Though the company leadership needs to monitor progress of the projects closely, it needs to get out of the way once they have the right team in place and then ensure that the teams get the resources they need.

FOSTERING COLLABORATION THROUGH COMMUNICATION NETWORKS

The best people with the best ideas need to be connected, regardless of where they are located on the globe or in the corporate hierarchy.

But silos are a fact of life. Companies are built like elevators.

Information travels up and down the hierarchy and rarely moves across silos with much ease. That's a problem, because innovation demands serendipity and connecting beyond the neighboring cubicles or departments. People need to reach out and touch someone who might have an insight, an idea, or useful information. This is where social networks come in. Not Facebook, but internal social networks that companies can create to link people across boundaries, helping them share knowledge and expertise.

In a recent conversation at the Kellogg School, the CEO of Boeing, Jim McNerney, described how Boeing was using technology to get its tens of thousands engineers to collaborate across boundaries. Boeing's engineers sometimes have simple questions: How can I locate someone who knows a lot about a specific topic? How can I learn whether what I'm doing has already been done? How can I find out if someone else is using the same technology across work groups? Though the questions are simple, the answers may lie with a person buried deep in a remote department thousands of miles away.

Boeing's solution is inSite, an intranet site where every employee has an identity and can establish a profile, much as people do on Facebook and LinkedIn. The site serves as a central location to find people, ask questions, publish thoughts, and share information. Most important, inSite provides a fertile breeding ground for Communities of Practice—groups of experts who share an area of expertise. Within four years of inSite's 2009 launch, eighty-three thousand Boeing employees were using the network regularly. One specific example illustrates the power of collaborative networks. At 7:38 in the evening on January 28, 2010, a user from Washington asked a question: "How can I best map large tools on a floor parking stall map?" At 3:00 the next morning, a user from Southern California answered the question. Washington posted additional comments at 7:25 A.M. Two hours later, someone in Virginia confirmed the answer. In all, within twenty-four hours, employees had passed knowledge across the company. More important, the knowledge was captured and documented for everyone in Boeing to access in the future.

Boeing's inSite network can be accessed whenever needed for a wide range of purposes. But collaborative networks can be more structured and purpose driven when they are organized around a brand, an innovation initiative, or a market. For instance, Microsoft has a community of Digital Leads— experts in digital and social media in different subsidiaries worldwide who come together both physically and virtually to define the frontiers of social media marketing for the company. Kraft has organized collaborative networks around categories, which it calls Global Category Teams. The GCTs lead the strategy development for biscuits, gum and candy, and so on. These teams manage select projects that need leveraging through expertise and scale in the spirit of *Fewer, Bigger, Bolder.* They also provide a worldwide category lens in contrast to the more narrowly focused country lens where the P&L resides. (Sometimes the views through the two lenses provide different perspectives that need to be resolved. More hard choices.)

Establishing and maintaining collaborative networks entail

discipline by leadership and—as at every stage in our program—relentless focus. Let's look at some principles to help make these networks work.

PRINCIPLES FOR COLLABORATIVE NETWORKS

Collaborative networks—the kind designed to incubate projects, not simply serve as communication systems—often get linked to big, international companies. But they can be even more important for start-ups. In those cases, the founders may be one or two strong, and their collaboration is with external experts and suppliers. A three-person start-up in Haddonfield, New Jersey, for example, needs to connect to an IT company in Israel and a factory in China. The principles—particularly regarding carefully setting out roles and responsibilities—remain the same. Here are some of the key ones:

Clarity—Within the collaborative network, there needs to be utter clarity on who does what and where responsibility lies. That includes making clear up front who has the authority to approve what. Early on, working with the company leadership, the network should create a template that establishes roles. The document should get granular—responsibilities and timetables laid out carefully—though the network members should take care not to obsess and spend too much time fussing over details. (Watch out for the typical responsibility assignment matrix—the so-called RAM or RACI. Filling out a complex format can easily become an end in itself.) Once the template is established, the core project team should monitor progress closely.

Flexibility—The one-two punch of digitalization and globalization has pretty much knocked out the importance of where an office is located and made way for the possibility—even necessity—for flexible schedules. People can work from anywhere, including their homes. All they need is to be connected. Of course, some activities need a center—product research, for example, usually requires a lab—but most projects don't need to be anchored at the home office. The days worked and even the hours don't have to follow rigid patterns. Obviously, with team members sometimes located in opposite time zones, some flexibility in work hours can't be avoided.

Of course, when the staff works at home, the company loses the face-to-face effect—the supposed creative spark that comes from employees sitting down together or serendipitously meeting and chatting around the water cooler. Still, the occasional spark produced in-office probably gets more than outweighed by the advantages of keeping talented people on the roster and contented. In any case, as the workforce gets more comfortable with advancing video communication technology, the creative sparks will continue to flow virtually.

Diversity—This word has been tossed around so casually that a fundamental point sometimes gets overlooked: Diversity is a competitive advantage. It brings different perspectives, insights, and styles to the table. In the most basic business terms, it expands the marketplace of ideas—lets them compete to see which is best. In a global environment, diversity stands for variety among nationalities, cultures, sexes, races—the huge range of perspectives can only enhance decision making. One of Sanjay's early bosses at Unilever, Robert M. Phillips, told his managers at the first meeting: "If all of you are going to agree with me, I don't want any of you."

Though women have moved into the business world at a heartening pace over the last few decades, they aren't moving up the corporate ranks at anywhere near the rate they should. It's the job of corporate leaders to change that and push for inclusion. Adding women to the mix is based on sound business principles. Their perspective and style are inevitably valuable. Of course, they bring talent and skills to the table at least equal to those of the men in the room. But sometimes the advantage can be subtle. Sanjay got a telling and funny glimpse of this at a leadership dinner not long after he joined Kraft. A man who was still adjusting to the company's new style stood and started ponderously describing the many virtues of his unit. Eyes rolled. Finally, Diane Johnson May, the personable but straight-talking head of human relations for Kraft Developing Markets, spoke up—she told him to shut up and sit down. He meekly followed her command, and everyone in the room laughed. Her remark changed the mood at the dinner dramatically, defusing the tension and formality. The gathered leaders got on with the work of moving the company forward. To this day, Sanjay believes that if a male had interrupted the man with an order to shut up, the reaction would have been different—egos would be bumping, tempers would flare. But May took in the situation and had the understanding and style to resolve it.

Family—We have touched on this principle several times in these pages, but it holds particular relevance in the realm of collaborative networks, where the fundamental idea is to work together. The unit is like a family. It is interdependent. Decisions are made with give-and-take, and once they are made, the group moves forward with consensus. Most companies are transactional, and individuals spend a lot of energy pushing through their ideas. There's an emphasis on lines of reporting—solid and dotted—and people waste time figuring them out. Authority and responsibility should be clear, but the atmosphere should be open for help and advice.

In a collaborative network there are no individual winners or losers. The members win or lose as a family.

Compensation—Workers in a collaborative network often get pulled away from their regular jobs, so questions of compensation sometimes come up. This shouldn't be difficult. The terms should be set out clearly in advance, but the base compensation of an individual doesn't need to change unless he or she is moving up in the larger organization. However, the network member should collect bonuses based on hitting milestones in the project.

Resistance—Despite the tremendous push given collaborative networks by digitalization and globalization, the practice still meets occasional resistance. Often, people are simply more comfortable staying within their silos—what they are used to—particularly when projects end or management changes. Leadership's job is to keep pushing against the resistance—continuing to appoint collaborative teams, monitoring the results, and spreading the word. Network collaboration is not going away, and everyone from the CEO to the worker on the line will have to learn to adjust—and to gain from it.

GOING GLOCAL

GLOCAL: Balance Between Mindlessly Global and Hopelessy Local

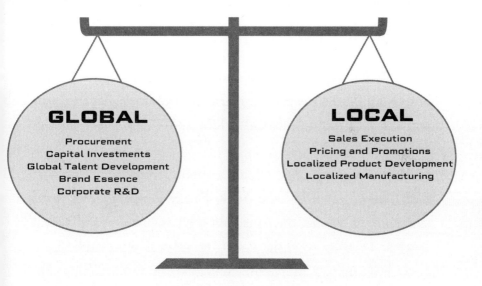

GLOBAL

Procurement
Capital Investments
Global Talent Development
Brand Essence
Corporate R&D

LOCAL

Sales Execution
Pricing and Promotions
Localized Product Development
Localized Manufacturing

Collaborative networks are the fundamental organizational tool for a company with global reach, but global companies struggle with another organizational challenge—how to balance a company's global resources with its local expertise. The proper balance represents the Holy Grail of *glocal* management—the ideal blend of both global and local strengths.

The first step in finding that balance is to take the blinders off. Business history is littered with examples of companies that took a popular domestic product and dropped it into another country, only to have it disappear into a black hole because of underestimated cultural differences. For example, Gillette blundered a decade ago with low-cost razors in India because it did not realize that many lower-income Indian men don't have access to running water when they shave, causing shaving cream to clog their razors. This sort of approach is mindlessly global.

At the other extreme, some international companies have virtually gone native in some places, turning their backs on the strength and expertise of the mother ship. They acquire local brands and build deep local market capabilities that then operate as a collection of local fiefdoms. We call this approach hopelessly local.

Here's a small, but telling example from Sanjay's years with Unilever. In 1987, the Anglo-Dutch conglomerate bought Chesebrough-Pond's, the American company famous for its skin creams. Then as now, the Pond's brand was represented by a sweet little tulip, a simple mnemonic for aid in marketing. But after assorted expansions around the world, Pond's had more than fifty different tulips gracing its packaging. The cost of supporting that huge bouquet wasn't enormous, but it did serve as a vivid example of how Pond's was going off in various directions, spending money, while, meantime, the brand was suffering.

Eventually, the company unified the brand under the umbrella of the Pond's Institute, a grouping that symbolized the expertise of Pond's worldwide. Then the company leadership took the practical approach of balancing global expertise with local products and local execution. The arrangement proved highly successful—Pond's grew faster than the market and was profitable. And as part of the overall unifying process, the little tulip was broadly harmonized across markets.

The key is to find the sweet spot between mindlessly global and hopelessly local. That's going glocal. The idea is to combine global expertise with local context so that you can get the benefits of scale from the corporate side and the benefits of market knowledge from the local side. Agree up front on what is to be done where and who has authority for what. Don't just take a middle road. The balance will depend on the particular project.

On the local side, the people on the front lines of the business are closest to the ground. They know—or should know—the tastes, habits, and attitudes of consumers. They have experience with the business practices in the locality, the infrastructure, and the pitfalls.

On the global side, aspects of the business that cross borders should hold sway. With technology, for example—there's nothing local about the fundamental models of technology. Consider how mobile phones and social networks have swept the globe. Facebook is more global than the United Nations! Several other aspects of business are best managed globally. Brand positioning. Safety issues regarding a product or the workplace. The rules and values of the company. These are matters that should apply generally over the globe.

Find the proper balance and stay with it. Adjust as needed, of course, but don't shift back and forth from one extreme to the other. International consumer products companies have a particularly bad history of making pendulum swings from highly global to highly local and back again, a proclivity that's disruptive and counterproductive.

Going glocal isn't evaluative—it doesn't judge what's good or what's bad. It simply demands a careful analysis of what should be done globally and what should be done locally. To illustrate how that analysis works in the real world, let's turn again to the case of Oreo in China. As Kraft prepared to re-launch the cookie in that huge market, the Oreo collaborative network team—led by the head of Oreo brand equity, based in New Jersey—created a list of all the potential drivers of prof-itable growth. For each driver, the team then decided whether the guiding hand would be local or global. Here's that list and the accompanying analysis:

1. Positioning—For years, Oreo had been defined by the slogan "Milk's Favorite Cookie" and by the ritual of twist, lick, dunk. The collaborative network team asked itself: Was that specific and traditional identity a fundamental element of the brand—a global thing—that should apply worldwide where Oreos are sold? Or should Oreo's positioning be left to local marketing? The answer wasn't obvious. The Chinese don't drink much milk, for one thing, and they'd have no idea what was meant by twist, lick, dunk. Still, in the end the network decided that the positioning should remain global—that there was a simplicity to creating and owning the ritual of twist, lick, dunk that people would easily grasp and that was unique. The power of Oreo's established positioning should not be dissipated. Based on that decision, the collaborative network put together some simple guidelines to be used globally for depicting Oreo's close association with milk and the twist, lick, dunk maneuver.

2. **Advertising execution**—If the positioning was global, should the advertising be global, too? That would certainly be cost effective—one basic ad used everywhere. But the team decided that the execution should remain local. Though the positioning guidelines helped anchor the fundamental elements, the actual ads would be produced locally and could differ around the globe. The logic was basic: Local people know the local market best. They could execute with local nuances within the twist, lick, dunk arena. Local control led to Kraft China hiring Yao Ming.

It is often helpful to put countries in clusters based on their stages of development for the brand. The approach taken to advertising execution can often be similar across a cluster.

3. **Product**—Should the actual cookie be the same as in the United States or could it be different? Initially, the response came back that Oreo had to be Oreo, and you can't fiddle with it. Global standards had to apply. But as the team puzzled over the question, they came to see that the steadfast approach explained in large part why Oreo had been unsuccessful outside the United States for ninety-five years. So the team drew up some basic global guidelines. The key ingredients needed to be the same—the same

chocolate, for example—but you could alter the level of sweetness according to local tastes. Similarly, you could alter the size, which opened the way to meeting more appropriate price points locally. In China, giving the local tastes control also led to innovations such as Oreo with filling flavored by green tea.

4. **Procurement**—This was relatively easy to decide: The purchase of key ingredients would be done globally or regionally, whatever made commercial sense.

5. **Technology**—As discussed above, this was global.

6. **Processing**—The team decided that the standards for how you mix and actually make the cookie should be handled globally. In fact, in China and elsewhere, Kraft Developing Markets discovered that various local techniques had been built into manufacturing processes for assorted Kraft products and often they introduced waste.

7. **Sales**—Sales were considered local, giving the folks closest to the market the chance to apply their insights. The team realized, however, that some of the sales strategies developed in China could be leveraged across other countries, so it formed another collaborative network to monitor and spread best practices (and also to ensure that sales practices among countries didn't become too fragmented).

8. **Capital**—Capital decisions should be made globally. The perspective on where to expend capital has to be broad. So, for example, the decision on where to locate a factory should come from the global handlers. They are best situated to put together all the pieces of the puzzle and to have a handle on the best practices from anywhere.

It's worth thinking of going glocal as a metaphor—a term that suggests a balancing of capabilities (whether the context is global or not). The Oreo folks captured the essentials: First, they defined the growth levers of the cookie. Then they agreed up front on what's going to be done where and who would be in charge. They aligned resources accordingly. With roles and actions clearly defined, they launched the initiative. The next step was to measure progress—establish metrics—which we will consider in the next chapter.

One final word on a successful organization, which comes as a note of caution on the role of corporate executives venturing from headquarters: Leaders often entertain the genuine sense that they have the talent to help. And usually they do. It's important to be careful of the tendency, however. Sometimes they parachute into a situation, which often turns into an unintended insult to the locals, and then they fly off again, leaving behind a frazzled team and a lot of words, but not much accomplishment. This exercise in wasted effort doesn't always happen, but despite the best of intentions, leaders probably fall into the trap too often. For years, Sanjay experienced it from the local side, scrambling to accommodate top-tier visitors. And then he stepped into a head office role. The trap is much harder to identify from that vantage point, but he's certain he fell into it, too, at least occasionally. The fact is, all parts of an organization have a role, and all parts need to add value in all they do. They have to earn their right to exist. Every leader should remind himself or herself of that first thing every day.

STEP 6—ORGANIZATION:

ALIGN AND COLLABORATE

1. If the organization is working, don't mess with it—be boringly consistent and execute. Reorganize if needed, but avoid radical restructuring except as a last resort, because it can be disruptive and distracting. Don't keep changing for the sake of change.
2. Drive growth by aligning the organization with opportunities and building collaborative networks that cross boundaries, both internal and external.

3. To align the organization with opportunities, consider creating a focused group that is expressly designed to pursue growth opportunities.

4. To work around organizational silos, create collaborative networks—physical as well as virtual—that can improve the lateral flow of information across company boundaries.

5. International operations should maximize growth by going glocal—that is, balancing local talent, with its frontline knowledge of consumers, business practices, and other on-the-ground elements, with the mother ship's global expertise and resources.

CHAPTER 9

METRICS:
MEASURE AND COMMUNICATE PROGRESS

1. Discovery
Search for Growth

2. Strategy
Pick Your Bets

3. Rallying Cry
Rouse the Troops

4. People
Unleash Potential

5. Execution
Simplify and Delegate

6. Organization
Align and Collaborate

7. Metrics
Measure and Communicate Progress

FOCUS7

Assume that you are driving a Toyota Prius hybrid on a one-thousand-mile round-trip. On the way out, you test how many miles you can squeeze out of your fuel-efficient car. You keep your eyes fixed on the fuel consumption indicator to see how many miles per gallon (mpg) the car is getting. To improve the results, you anticipate stops, avoid extreme acceleration, and drive at no more than 55 miles per hour. By the end of the first leg, you achieve great mileage of 50 mpg, but your trip took ten hours. On the way back, you need to return fast. You keep your eyes fixed on your GPS display to see how many miles you have to go and when you are expected to arrive. You drive as fast as you can without getting a speeding ticket. You end up making the return trip in less than seven hours, but you only get 40 miles to the gallon.

This analogy contains several lessons about measuring progress. The first is that what you measure will depend on what you want to manage. If your goal is to use gas efficiently, you will measure gas consumption and try to optimize mileage. Similarly, if a company's growth goals emphasize revenue growth, the leadership's metrics will focus on the top line—market share and revenues. On the other hand, if the goal is to drive the bottom line, the metrics will focus on cost reduction, productivity, and operational efficiency.

The second lesson is that metrics need to be balanced. They can be backward looking (what we call "rearview mirror" metrics) or they can be forward looking ("windshield" metrics). Gas mileage is a rearview mirror metric because it measures the average *past* fuel consumption. In contrast, current speed and time to the destination are forward-looking metrics because they focus on the present and the future. If you just focus on mpg, you end up with a trip that takes too long. If you just focus on how fast you are driving, you may end up using a lot of fuel. The point is to find the right balance for the task you are measuring.

The third and probably most important lesson is that the simpler your metrics, the easier it is to manage them. Even if the amount of gas a car consumes depends on a complex combination of factors—the speed, driving conditions, level of traffic congestion, ambient temperature, tire pressure, and driving style—isolate the few that best tell you what you need to know.

Progress shouldn't simply be measured, however—it also needs to be communicated through stories of success. While metrics express plainly how a company is doing, telling stories about the triumphs (and occasional failures) inspires and motivates people. Metrics that quantify progress appeal to the mind. Stories that celebrate success appeal to the heart. A successful company satisfies both aspects by providing both metrics and stories, connecting with both the mind and the heart. Let's start with how you can apply the principles of focus and simplicity to the measurement of progress.

GROUND METRICS IN GOALS

As the Cat explains to Alice on her trip through Wonderland, if you don't know where you're going, then it doesn't matter which way you go. To know your milestones, you need to know where you are going. Metrics owe their origin to the goals that a company sets for itself. The choice of metrics, therefore, is directly connected to the goals you select.

Consider the experience of VMock, the start-up résumé company that we talked about in chapter 7. Fundamentally,

VMock needed to ask itself: How do we define progress? What metrics should we manage to? The most logical metric that businesses focus on is revenues. After all, what could be more logical than saying that you want to grow the business and keep your attention focused on growing the top line? So VMock came up with a model for licensing its résumé analysis and career preparation platform to universities, charging them a fee based on the number of students who used the platform. Unfortunately, the universities balked at paying licensing fees, and the adoption of VMock's platform was slower than the company's expectations.

At a strategy meeting, Mohan and VMock founder Salil Pande realized that the company was defining progress incorrectly by measuring in revenue dollars because price had become a barrier to customer adoption. In the online services business, they decided, progress—at least at the start—should be defined solely by the base of users on VMock's platform. Revenues would come later from sources such as advertising. Businesses such as Instagram, Waze, Twitter, Snapchat, and others like them have shown that multibillion-dollar valuations are sometimes based on little or no revenues, let alone profits! The game is about the number of eyeballs you attract. Snapchat, a company with zero revenues, turned down Facebook's acquisition offer of $3 billion in cash. Why? With more than four hundred million "snaps" being sent every day by its users, Snapchat thinks it is worth more. The revised definition of progress at VMock is simple: *Grow the user base at any cost, even if you give away the platform.* The goal the company has set for itself is equally simple: *Get to one million users as fast as possible.* Once you know where you want to go, the metrics become evident.

KEEP METRICS BALANCED

In coming up with a scorecard of performance and progress, it is important to have a set of balanced metrics. For instance, in the blank-check initiatives at Kraft, the metrics include revenues as well as gross profit margins. This ensures that the teams did not pursue revenue growth without worrying about profit margins or pursue profits alone at the expense of revenues. Checks and balances are critical in coming up with a good portfolio of metrics.

The most commonly used metrics in business today tend to revolve around sales and profits. In fact, the essence of business performance is top-line and bottom-line growth. But the best measures of *performance* are not the best measures of *progress,* a scale that often comes into play when measuring innovative projects. Performance shows what the company did in the past. Progress is an estimate of how the company will do in the future. To measure progress on innovation initiatives, you need to make sure your metrics are forward looking.

Let's look at how Whirlpool Corporation does this. According to Moisés Noreña, the global director of innovation at Whirlpool, the company has an Innovation Dashboard that consists of three basic metrics. The first focuses on measuring the number and value of projects in the innovation pipeline (iPipeline). At this stage, Whirlpool estimates the potential value of an innovation project once it is introduced to the market. The second metric is innovation revenue (iRevenue), which measures the revenue generated by an innovative product after it hits the market. The third metric is the External Operating Profit Lift (EOP Lift), which measures the differential margins that the innovation produces relative to Whirlpool's base business. By looking ahead through the iPipeline, Whirlpool is able to estimate the future business impact of its innovation projects.

Metrics also need to be balanced across the different stages in a growth and innovation project. Boeing's Jim McNerney elegantly articulated this idea on his visit to the Kellogg School. Based on his experience as the CEO of 3M Corporation and Boeing, he had found that a company tends to have two stages in its innovation process. The earlier stage is for development of ideas and concepts. At this stage, the process needs to be managed for *flow* of ideas. When the ideas go into development, however, money is spent and they become products. At this stage, the metrics need to adapt and the process needs to be managed for *yield*. Managing a process for creativity and flow is very different from managing a process for discipline and yield. The metrics you need in the two processes are exact opposites of each other. Using yield metrics to manage a creative process will choke off the flow of ideas. Conversely, using flow metrics to manage a capital-intensive product development process can lead to chaos. Keeping a company balanced is one of the biggest leadership challenges, according to Mc-Nerney.

KEEP METRICS SIMPLE

Consider this dismaying account: The company was getting by, but it wasn't breaking ground and it wasn't making strides. In fact, the rate of growth had been declining for more than five years. Concerned about the sluggish pace, the enterprising CEO ordered up a company-wide assessment—an exhaustive, unit-by-unit survey across a broad array of fronts. For every objective, he wanted a measurement; for every number, an explanation. With the help of consultants, the survey took almost six months to create. Although some questions applied to the entire organization, many were particular to the business of a specific unit. When finally drawn up, the survey stretched to fifteen pages long.

The document landed on the desks of managers in early December, and with a frenzy of e-mails and late nights, every unit responded by the end of the month, despite the tumult of the holiday season. The CEO sent managers a note of thanks on New Year's Day.

It took several months for teams of financial people and consultants to assimilate the information, and then more months of meetings and discussions for the company leadership to puzzle over what the assessment told them. Eventually, the CEO pronounced that the assessment had provided a helpful snapshot of where the company stood, but he and his aides concluded that many aspects of the business had not been adequately explored. They made up a list of additional questions. Because the original assessment was now more than six months out of date, the company decided to conduct another year-end assessment, adding the new questions. The results followed the same pattern, but the CEO and his aides concluded that they were gaining useful knowledge. They decided to make the assessment an annual event.

Unfortunately, five years after that first assessment, and despite the reams of information collected, the company's business had turned from sluggish to stalled. Revenues were down, costs up. In fact, the only aspect of the entire operation that had shown robust growth was the survey questionnaire—which now came in at a healthy twenty-five pages long.

The company in that sad account represents a composite of several companies, but the underlying story is dangerously familiar and illustrates a pitfall common to countless organizations: setting too many objectives and then ordering up too many ways to measure them. Overambitious metrics serve as a prime example of directing attention internally, instead of externally—the syndrome of looking in a mirror rather than looking through the window at the outside world.

This number crunching can have several pernicious consequences. For one, although information may well be power, it has to be the *right information*. A blizzard of nonvital facts and figures will merely clog the system and slow everything down. Another downside: An assessment like that described here wastes time and money all up and down the ranks. And it can become obsessive—an end in itself. Efforts that could be expended in building the business get lost in gathering data and filling out forms. Worse, the effort to explain results, explain trends, explain *the past* becomes a primary objective. Hours of potentially productive time are frittered away talking about what has happened, not *Karna Kya Hai?*—*"So what do we do now?"*

Here's a good indication that your system of metrics has gone horribly wrong: You spend more time in reporting and analysis than in actually taking action.

The fundamental point with metrics is to keep things simple. Measurement and benchmarking are vitally important, but they should be basic and easily comprehensible, able to be scanned at a glance. Adding too many numbers only adds complexity to the operation. The abundance distracts from the measures that really matter, and it confuses priorities. The guideline: Hold scorecards to a single page, no more. And don't forget the Five Finger Rule—stray beyond it, and you're wasting everybody's time.

HOW TO FORMULATE YOUR METRICS

The numbers on your scorecard need to connect directly to the strategic objectives—they need to indicate clearly your progress toward your established goals. Put another way: You need to measure what you are supposed to be doing. Beyond that, metrics should come with milestones attached. At what point is a specific goal supposed to be achieved? And the measurements should be established within the framework—short-term/long-term, quarterly, annually, et cetera.

We recommend formulating metrics around three questions:

1. *What* do we measure?
2. *When* do we measure it?
3. *Who* gets involved?

As we have discussed earlier in this chapter, the *What* needs to relate directly to the strategic goals. Kraft Foods asked business managers to fill out a one-page scorecard that included three key measures: sales, profits, and cash flow. Those metrics were aimed at relatively high-level managers and concerned the overall strength of the business. Different levels of management will see different things. For units with specific roles, the measures also would be different—though the basic principles should remain the same across functions. Above all, simplicity reigns. For example, for measuring the effectiveness of a salesperson in the developing markets traditional trade (mom-and-pop stores), the score might include coverage (number of outlets covered), productivity, and revenue per productive outlet.

The *When* depends on the function or company context. Reports can be weekly, monthly, or quarterly. There is no necessary rule to follow, other than that the metrics should come with milestones attached—when will a particular stage be accomplished—and they should be benchmarked, always against an annual plan, usually against a five-year plan.

Who gets involved requires the careful delegation of authority. This has particular relevance for the top bosses. How far down should their knowledge of particular performance results reach, or, put another way, how far up should the granular results of a piece of the business stretch? One thing to remember: The more people involved, the more complexity expands.

Take, for example, a sales manager in a large organization. Who follows the metrics of his performance? We suggest basically two people: the sales manager and his boss. In general, senior executives should not reach down, leapfrogging a layer or two of management. When they do reach, there's usually no malice involved—just an inherent belief that the big bosses can add value, particularly when problems arise. But by intruding, the executive upends the regular hierarchy. Pretty soon everyone at all levels gets involved, scurrying to explain what happened. Resources get wasted. Efforts turn internal. Focus gets clouded. If people are not doing what they need to do against metrics, someone has to take action. But if, say, the CEO reaches three or four levels down, the attention turns inward, and then success comes to be defined as pleasing senior management.

Of course, the occasional exception may make sense—once in a while, a higher-up may tap in to show she's staying on top of things and to keep people on their toes. But if senior management repeatedly asks questions a few levels down, the managers below are likely to spend more time cobbling and sanitizing answers and less time doing productive work.

The situation is different if the point is to deliver a compliment. The CEO, say, can send a note to the sales manager congratulating him on great results, with maybe a copy to his boss. Along the same lines, sending out a note to a wider audience pointing out a success can be a wonderfully effective motivator through the vehicle of positive shame. For example, say you are presiding over five markets. Circulating a table comparing productivity for each market can have a powerful effect on the people running each. Everyone wants to be at the top of the list. No one wants to dwell at the bottom.

COMMUNICATING PROGRESS THROUGH STORYTELLING

Metrics are obviously important. Numbers don't lie. They provide a stark measure of how a company, a unit, an employee is doing. But numbers are only part of the game.

Progress is also measured in events and incidents that are relevant to the company's goals and that touch the emotions of stakeholders. To make a point, to teach a lesson, to inspire the troops, nothing compares with telling a story—providing a memorable, engaging anecdote or report of happenings. People have probably been entertaining each other with stories almost since *Homo sapiens* first found his voice. Scientists have demonstrated how our brains are wired for storytelling. We tend to think in terms of narratives—stories give meaning to our experiences; they help us assimilate information and remember facts. Raw numbers on a screen tend to slip through our memories. But drop a key number into a narrative and it's got the grip of context to stay with us. "Stories are the creative conversion of life itself into a more powerful, clearer, more meaningful experience," the teacher and screenwriter Robert McKee has said. "They are the currency of human contact."

Let's put it more bluntly: Stories stick. People remember stories. No one remembers mind-numbing PowerPoint slides.

A smart manager uses storytelling as a key mechanism to lead, but the story has to be well chosen. Many people in business are more comfortable with numbers than with anecdotes, so they rely too heavily on numbers and lose the audience. That's trouble, but the opposite can be trouble, too—an anecdote that's so light on substantiation that it floats off, unremembered. Unless you are telling a parable, the best stories are usually bolstered by details and facts—not so many as to overwhelm, but enough to anchor the story in reality.

The key point: Every story has to have a purpose. The idea isn't to entertain. Ultimately, the story should point toward action to change the business trajectory, while inspiring the talent in the company.

Everyone from Harvard's John Kotter to documentarian Ken Burns to novelist Leo Tolstoy have talked about the power of storytelling, and many have written about its dynamic effect in a business setting. Sanjay made storytelling an essential element in the Focus7 framework. We've already discussed how congratulatory tales at the dinners after discovery workshops can be used to raise spirits and encourage others to do better. Accounts of blank-check efforts can be terrifically instructive throughout an organization: What were the lessons learned? Can the insights gained in one unit be applied to other aspects of the business? "The analysis of the blank-check initiatives in write-ups and discussions was one of the most effective teaching tools we had at Kraft," says Pradeep Pant, president of Kraft Asia Pacific. "In many instances, the lessons can be put to direct use. Other times, the analysis simply sets off analogous thinking."

The use of storytelling reached a crescendo at Kraft in October 2012, when Sanjay's team organized a conference built entirely around telling stories. Some four hundred leaders from more than sixty countries gathered for two and a half days in Istanbul. The instruction to participating units and leaders was elemental: Tell us about your accomplishments, so we can learn and be inspired—but do it without speechifying, PowerPoint, and the usual conference tedium. Sanjay didn't know what to expect. He didn't vet the scripts ahead of time, and he required only that each presentation include a section on what we do next. This conference was not intended to be all feel-good and fluff. It was supposed to provide inspiration and lead to action.

For two and a half days, the teams basically put on shows—using innovative and captivating techniques to tell their stories and make their points. One man, Kraft's head in Ghana, emerged onstage in full tribal regalia, complete with towering headgear. Making a point about how reaching out to the community can attract talent, he explained that he came from an uneducated family and worked on a cocoa plantation until Cadbury invested in his education and provided sanitary services to his village.

The Chinese team showcased so-called Hope Kitchens, a community service initiative aimed at rural China under which the company has provided meals to fifty thousand children while helping to educate teachers and kitchen workers on the elements of good diets. The fundamental idea is that you can do good while doing well—the initiative has been hugely powerful in winning the war for talent in China, attracting a long roster of top performers who wanted to give back to their communities.

The conference reached a dramatic high point when Barbara Miranda, head of Kraft's business in northeast Brazil, wearing a colorful native dress, called Sanjay to the stage to help tie threads on a spear, a traditional regional ritual. The ceremony highlighted a remarkable success story: In an impoverished area of the region, Kraft in just eighteen months had converted underdeveloped fields into a huge factory complex that provided local employment and other investments in the community. Meantime, the business unit of northeast Brazil was blowing sales, profit, and cash targets out of the water.

Miranda's presentation brought tears to the eyes of many in the audience but, more important, it illustrated the value of mining for gold—looking for opportunity in overlooked areas. The northeast Brazil experience offered a clear road map for action for other Kraft regional units.

At the conclusion of the conference, a London theater group hired for the occasion drew on the themes developed during the gathering to organize an extravaganza of a closing that involved all four hundred attendees in song-and-dance routines. A survey conducted afterward found that many participants said it was the most useful and engaging business conference they had ever attended.

The Istanbul conference turned into a ballyhooed success within Kraft, in part because it started by taking people out of their comfort zone, the world of metrics alone. (Among those discomforted at first was Sanjay, who had a few sleepless nights worrying whether the conference was a risk too far.) But pushing authority down, relying on the troops to teach and inspire one another, proved to be a triumph.

It would be dangerously easy to get carried away with this. Talk can be cheap and, in the end, numbers count. That's why stories about failure should also be told. Leaders are far from infallible, and that point should be embraced.

Reality is a vital quality. Life goes through good and bad, businesses endure ups and downs. Many business leaders (and their communication departments) forget this and insist on staying relentlessly positive, and ignoring or spinning difficult news. Employees can see through this, and the Panglossian treatment insults them. As we have said, candor pays off. This is a key element of Focus7: Own up to your mistakes. Admit them. Teach with them. Stories of failure can be wonderfully instructive.

But the key is to keep moving forward, measuring your progress with both numbers and stories, connecting to both the mind and the heart.

STEP 7—METRICS:

MEASURE AND COMMUNICATE PROGRESS

1. Measure progress with numbers that quantify, inform, and speak to the mind. At the same time, communicate progress through stories that instruct, compliment, inspire, and speak to the heart.
2. Metrics need to be grounded in strategic goals—what you measure depends on what you want to manage and achieve.
3. Metrics need to be simple—measure only a few things that really matter so that people know what the game is and how you are keeping score.

4. Metrics need to be balanced so that you measure different facets of progress and are forced to consider trade-offs among the different facets.

5. Progress needs to be communicated through stories that celebrate success and help foster a culture of winning in the organization.

CHAPTER 10

AVOIDING THE PITFALLS

Taking on Focus7 promises substantial, lasting rewards. But, as with any transformation, there are hazards that may thwart you along the way. Here are five pitfalls that we have seen in developing growth initiatives and tips on how to sidestep them.

1. FIX BEFORE YOU SCALE

Imagine that you are driving a car that has serious steering and brake problems. What's likely to happen if you step on the gas? A calamitous accident. So it is with growth initiatives. Too often, companies drop massive resources into initiatives that are fundamentally flawed. At the end of the day, growth has to be profitable and sustainable—if you don't have a robust and validated business model, you can end up losing your shirt. What's more, if you have a mess, scaling up a mess just leads to a bigger mess. The point: Get the model right before you scale up. Test, learn, adapt, iterate. Once you have evidence that the model works, then step on the gas.

A number of multinational companies have made the mistake of investing in emerging markets without a workable plan. We've described how Kraft poured millions into China on little more than the hope that the huge size and the rapid growth of the market would somehow pay off. But only after the products, distribution channels, and marketing communications were fine-tuned did the business actually take off. Some multinationals never made it that far. China has proved to be a Waterloo for many. The Dutch grocery chain Ahold, for example, opened forty supermarkets in China, but sold off after five years of a fruitless search for profits. Similarly, the Italian dairy company Parmalat gave up after discovering that it couldn't compete with local operations.

Scaling before fixing is particularly dangerous if you are moving into uncharted waters—new customer segments, capabilities, geographies, distribution channels, and (increasingly in the online services world) business models. Every major technology company is rushing into the cloud services business because they want to emulate the success of companies like Salesforce.com, Amazon.com, Dropbox, Workday, and Service-Now. But making money on cloud services is far from a sure thing—the traditional system of selling software licenses is going out the window, replaced by innovations such as the freemium model (paid upgrades from a free version) and by advertising-subsidized services.

We see history repeating itself from the dot-com era, when

there was a similar rush to get big fast with untried and untested business models. Take, for example, Pandesic, a ballyhooed joint venture between two technology titans, Intel and SAP. Founded in late 1997, Pandesic offered "e-commerce in a box" by combining Intel-based computers preloaded with SAP's market-leading business software suite for a paltry up-front fee of $25,000. The company planned to make most of its money by extracting up to 6 percent of the revenues that its customers would make from their e-commerce businesses. The fatal flaw: Pandesic attracted a bunch of dubious e-commerce start-ups as customers. It gave them millions of dollars of subsidies, hoping to capture revenues down the road. But many of the start-ups failed, and the revenues never materialized. On top of the flawed business model, Pandesic's SAP software was ill suited to e-commerce and required a lot of support. Instead of testing its venture on a small scale, Pandesic pressed on with big investments in sales, deployment, and customer support. Within three years, Pandesic went out of business and shut down after burning through almost $200 million in capital.

Here's the simple admonition: If your strategy doesn't promise profitable, sustained growth when you plant a flag in a new market or embark on a new venture, don't invest massive resources in mindless expansion. Test, learn, and scale up only when you see a clear path to sustained, profitable growth.

2. DON'T NEGLECT NONPRIORITY BUSINESSES

In the Focus7 approach, we have emphasized the need to allocate disproportionate resources and attention to priority businesses— whether these are brands, markets, products, or customer segments. But that leads to a question: What happens to the nonpriority businesses? Do we treat them as orphans? Get rid of them? Simply shedding these businesses as an act of "cutting off the tail" can be disastrous for several reasons. The growth of the priority businesses may not compensate for the lost revenues from the businesses you cut back. The nonpriority businesses may share fixed costs and assets with the priority businesses that may be difficult to disentangle. Employees may have strong emotional ties to nonpriority businesses.

To avoid this pitfall, we recommend the following steps:

1. Cluster the nonpriority businesses into four categories based on profit and growth potential—high versus low *profit potential* and high versus low *growth potential.* Recognize that each of these categories needs to be managed for different goals and with different resources and skills.
2. Manage nonpriority businesses that have high growth potential (even if profitability is currently in question) as *quasi-start-ups* run at arm's length by autonomous teams.
3. Manage nonpriority businesses that have low growth potential but high profitability as *cash cows* with minimal investments.

4. Sell off or shut down businesses that have low profit and low growth potential—these are the true *dogs*.

Kraft's Vegemite business in Australia, for example, is a local jewel—very profitable in its market, but with limited wider appeal. As we've seen, though Vegemite did not make it to the list of priority brands, Kraft retained it in the portfolio and delegated much of the responsibility for the business to a local team with little oversight by regional or global company leaders. Businesses like Vegemite often help provide scale in manufacturing and help defray overhead expenses. Local jewels like Vegemite should be managed like distinct entities—left alone to determine their own destiny but held accountable for revenues, margins, and cash flow.

The nonpriority businesses that throw off cash but don't hold much promise for growth should be managed for cash, again with limited senior management attention and limited new investments. Perhaps increase the price or reduce costs to make money in the short run. Don't invest substantial resources. In fact, the point is to *divert* money and even talent from these businesses to the priorities.

As for the dogs, the businesses that don't make money and aren't expected to grow or make money, here's a classic symptom: Time after time, your turnaround efforts have failed, with promises of growth and profits always seeming to shift a little further into the future. These businesses need to be divested in a disciplined manner over a defined time frame.

Consider Fonterra Brands' dairy business in Mexico. Though

Mexico is a developing market with growth potential, Fonterra's business model suffered underlying problems—the company had too many low-margin products and its cost structure was too high. An analysis concluded that the business could be fixed, but the resources and the time could be better deployed in other markets. Fonterra's leadership team decided to sell off the business. Making these hard choices is part of the Focus7 approach. Once a decision has been taken to sell a business, people with the relevant skills should be put on the transaction. In the case of Fonterra Brands, Mexico, a multifunctional task force (distinct from the folks managing the business on the ground) was set up and carried out the job.

AT&T's Yellow Pages business stands as another example of a nonpriority business that was dressed up for sale. The business was once a cash cow, generating fat profits year after year from local businesses that bought listings. But the Internet has dramatically eroded the Yellow Pages business—the fingers still "do the walking" (as the famous Yellow Pages tagline went) but today they walk on computer keyboards. Revenue had been plummeting, although the business was still profitable. In April 2012, AT&T sold off a majority stake in the Yellow Pages business to the private equity firm Cerberus Capital Management for $950 million. With this sale, AT&T was able to redeploy the cash to invest in the wireless business—a priority for AT&T.

Under Focus7, the priority businesses should grow and the nonpriority businesses should gradually become a smaller contributor to revenues and profits. But this process isn't instantaneous and it isn't neat. Hitting specific percentages or time frames should not become an end in itself, to be achieved at any cost. Let the process run its course, balancing practical execution with discipline.

3. CUT COSTS RUTHLESSLY BUT NOT MINDLESSLY

Keeping costs lean is a cornerstone of Focus7, and cuts provide fuel to invest behind priorities. While it is important to be ruthless about taking out costs that do not contribute to the focus initiatives, the trick is to be selective. We have seen two types of mindless cost cutting. One is the sequester approach, where companies slash costs across the board—announcing, for instance, that everyone takes a 10 percent cut! This is counterproductive because some aspects of the business deserve investment whether times are good or bad. The other type of mindless cost cutting is "sweating the small stuff"— spending inordinate effort going after small expenses, often setting up a cumbersome bureaucracy to monitor compliance. This ends up creating more noise than output.

Decide where cuts make sense. In particular, companies should tread with extreme care in cost cutting in three areas: investments in talent, in brands, and in customer care. Talent and brands are the most valuable assets for driving growth. We recommend increasing investments in hiring and developing talent, even ahead of the company's needs. By the same token, we recommend increasing investments in building brands even though brand investments pay off over a longer time frame than promotional spending. And customer care is crucial to customer satisfaction, so cutting back on service standards is a dangerous way to find savings. On the other hand, stay ruthless in cutting out superfluous work—or, at least, simplifying it. Businesses tend to get fat, so with thoughtful analysis, you can sometimes eliminate a whole layer of bureaucracy. The classic case comes with something such as reporting—how many reports need to go to whom and how often? Frequently, you find large numbers of people just feeding the internal beast.

To decide how much and where to cut, use benchmarking as your guide. Internal benchmarks are the easiest to do. A simple league table of comparison of costs among various business units can identify the outliers. In addition, external benchmarking (comparing yourself with other businesses, not necessarily from the same industry) can identify best in class and show what is possible.

How often should you benchmark? External benchmarking is something you can only do from time to time, because it is expensive and time-consuming. But internal benchmarking should be an ongoing process. How does a function in one unit compare with the same function in another? Take, for example, information technology, a function that can mushroom in large companies, as new businesses are acquired that bring different, incompatible IT systems. After Kraft acquired Cadbury, which owned IT systems that were redundant with Kraft's systems, Kraft's leadership decided it needed to standardize worldwide—the company was way out of whack with external benchmarks. Even though installing a new system throughout Kraft would be expensive, the effort would eventually cut costs and simplify the whole operation dramatically. So the company embarked on introducing a new system, but phased it in gradually to avoid disruption.

Meantime, though, Kraft continued to benchmark internally and found that the IT operations in Mexico and Australia were out of line with costs in similar units within Kraft. That led to more selective cuts, some generated by the local managers.

The good news is that Focus7 yields significant cost savings through elimination of management layers, reduction of overhead, and elimination of marginal business. Focus frees up resources that can be used to fuel growth.

4. STAY THE COURSE

Organizations are like people—they get easily bored and suffer from attention deficit disorder. They get tired of their strategy and want to make changes. Some like to embellish the strategy by introducing annual themes: This year's theme is innovation. Next year's is sales excellence. Then a financial pinch arrives and the theme becomes lean and mean. And on it goes. Gradually, the strategy gets confused and unfocused.

As we have argued throughout, changing strategy too often

creates disruption and distraction. Once a direction has been established, stay the course until the strategy has been fully implemented and had a chance to work its effect. This is not what we see in common practice. Companies tend to change strategies every few years, particularly after new leadership comes in. They spend months or even years planning a strategy, then quickly discard it and move on to something new. Growth through focus requires patience and perseverance. Stick with your strategy and don't take ad hoc steps. As we have said, plan shorter, but act longer. Again, we believe that 90 percent of your efforts should go into execution.

Prepare yourself for some trying discussions. People love the new, and that goes for bosses, too—new themes, new slogans, new strategies. Three years after Lipton introduced its Paint the World Yellow strategy, company leadership wanted to move on to something new. Sanjay and his colleagues argued that the strategy was only 20 percent implemented—it was on track and needed the time to reach its full potential. Ultimately, Lipton agreed and stayed the course, and Paint the World Yellow proved its mettle through years of brand leadership.

While the overall strategy needs to be steady while implementing Focus7, you should adapt tactics within the strategic framework. In a fast-paced and digitally connected world, the traditional, long-range approach to strategy development is dead. Annual budgets and strategic planning remain necessary, but the time spent formulating strategy needs to be reduced and the emphasis shifted to execution. The new approach to strategy emphasizes agility—constantly sensing opportunities and threats and responding in a fast, focused, and flexible manner. Tactics may adapt and shift, but the overall strategy should remain consistent and stable. This idea of "freedom within a framework"—agile execution within a delineated plan—is a thread that runs through Focus7 in strategy formulation, in organization design, and in the empowerment of people. Of course, if there is a market disruption or if the existing strategy is not delivering results consistently, then flexibility in strategy is essential.

5. DON'T PANIC WHEN THE GOING GETS TOUGH

The true test of leadership at any level comes when the going gets tough. And things do get tough. Indeed, if everything is always going well, something is wrong! But when trouble erupts, that's when the action orientation has to kick in, when you ask *Karna Kya Hai?*—"*So what do we do now?*"

When things turn bad, it's easy to get demoralized. The leadership's attitude turns sour, and the glum mood can infect the entire organization. The bosses typically respond by asking for more internal reviews, then more people review the internal reviews. Everyone tries to get involved. The noise jacks up and the entire operation turns internal, exactly the opposite of what's needed. Finally, the bosses take out an axe and start swinging away. Though cutting is not necessarily a bad response—as long as it's selective—the much more important point is to buck up the outlook before the transformation initiative gets derailed. Leaders need to face the facts and make the hard decisions. As we have said before, they owe candor to employees about the situation. But they have to strike a balance. Alongside the candor, they need to keep a positive tone and promote a can-do attitude throughout the business.

When things are tough, it is more important than ever to focus the business behind what matters. Delay all stuff that would simply be nice to do. An initiative overload is problematic at the best of times, and it can be lethal during periods of trouble.

It is important to have a sense of urgency but not a sense of fear. In fact, during bad times, leaders need to go out of their way to put their arms around key talent. Making scapegoats only adds to the atmosphere of fear and uncertainty. No one becomes a problem overnight.

The power of focus comes from its emphasis on what works. That's the mindset that should persist through good times and bad. It takes discipline and agility, certainly, and sometimes a fair amount of bravado, but staying on target with priorities is the surest way to weather almost any storm.

AVOIDING THE PITFALLS

FIVE
KEY
TAKEAWAYS

1. Before you proceed full tilt on a transformational growth initiative, carefully assess whether you have a robust business model in place—you need to fix the model before you scale.

2. Focusing on priority businesses does not mean ignoring nonpriority businesses. Segment the portfolio of nonpriority businesses into quasi-start-ups to be managed autonomously, cash cows to be milked for resources to fund growth, and dogs to be divested within a defined time frame.

3. Cost cutting is central to the Focus7 approach, but cut selectively, not mindlessly. With careful benchmarking,

focus cost cutting on areas that are bloated and bureaucratic and be cautious of cutting back on talent and brand assets.

4. Strategy needs to be given time to work—resist the temptation to jump on the next big thing. Within a consistent and clear strategic framework, however, stay agile in tactics and execution.

5. When you hit bumps in the road in Focus7 initiatives, don't panic—hold the larger picture in view. Leaders need to maintain an upbeat tone and keep the morale of the team high to get through the tough times.

CHAPTER 11

CREATING A
VIRTUOUS CYCLE

Our Focus7 journey consisted of seven steps. We started with gaining insights that led to the identification of a range of opportunities (Discovery). Using lenses, these opportunities were then narrowed down into a small set of big and bold initiatives that had the potential to generate profitable growth (Strategy). The journey continued with the expression of strategy through a call to arms that has the power to align and inspire people (Rallying Cry). Next, with the right people matched against priorities, the fewer, bigger, and bolder theme continued with our call to distort resources and bet disproportionately on a few high-potential teams that can drive a few carefully chosen blank-check initiatives (People). We made things happen by simplifying all facets of the operation and delegating decision making closer to customers (Execution). We also carried the theme of focus to the design of the organization, proposing that it be aligned with opportunities and made more collaborative by connecting people across silos (Organization). Finally, our journey called for keeping score through simple and focused metrics to measure performance and through rich and evocative storytelling to communicate progress (Metrics).

And so we come to the end, right? Wrong. The journey of Focus7 never ends—it's not a circle, but a spiral. A focused business keeps building on a sustainable foundation. Recall our caution that Focus7 isn't a one-time solution to be applied and then abandoned. On the contrary, the process (and steps in the process) belongs in the toolbox of every manager, used to keep the business nimble and constantly improving. Sometimes you'll have to pull out that toolbox in the middle of the night, so to speak. Your business will be humming along when a tremor suddenly hits. In fact—and this flies in the face of instinct—when trouble looms, usually in the form of pressure for short-term growth, that's exactly the moment to make bold bets. More on that in a moment.

Kraft Developing Markets used the Focus7 journey to go from years of underperformance to a surge in revenues—from $5 billion in 2006 to $16 billion in 2012. Though some of this growth came from acquisitions (Cadbury, Danone, etc.), the business saw sustained double-digit growth for six years—an impressive streak in the midst of one of the worst economic downturns the world has seen since 1929. What's more important than the *quantity* of growth, however, is the *quality* of the revenue growth. Revenues at Kraft Developing Markets showed a significant improvement in profitability and cash flow—in fact, profitability improved by 50 percent over this period. These results in turn created a spirit of winning that served as a magnet for talent, which was essential to fuel continued growth.

Relying on the principles of Focus7, Sanjay oversaw similar strong results at Fonterra Brands and Lipton. Mohan has seen similar results in his work with technology companies such as Bahwan CyberTek and VMock. In other words, Focus7 can be applied across industries, company size, and geography.

The goal of Focus7 and, indeed, the core message of our book, is to *sustain* profitable growth and in fact to accelerate it. As we've said, we are not searching for growth that relies on a one-time or short-term bump in revenues—a spike resulting from a huge price cut, for example. Rather, we are talking about growth that builds upon itself and fuels further growth. This idea—of creating a growth spiral—is what we call the Virtuous Cycle of Growth (see diagram). The Virtuous Cycle produces growth that is sustainable and comes with handsome profits—the kind of growth that matters.

The basics of the Virtuous Cycle parallel the steps in Focus7: You focus where you can win. You make bets in areas that yield higher gross margins, so your overall gross margin improves. You continually simplify processes and reduce costs based on benchmarking. And, throughout, you are always creating a cushion in your cash resources to accommodate the unforeseen—because unforeseen things will always happen.

The Virtuous Cycle requires two simple conditions to work: Grow the top line faster than the competition and grow the bottom line faster than the top line. As long as you can keep doing this, the Virtuous Cycle will keep humming along.

The pursuit of the Virtuous Cycle undergirds Focus7 and infuses our entire seven-step framework. Put another way, Focus7 deals with the *process.* The Virtuous Cycle represents the *outcome,* though the outcome continues to be driven by the Focus7 principles. Let's review the elements of the Virtuous Cycle.

FOCUS WHERE YOU CAN WIN

At the center of the focus process, leaders identify what will deliver the greatest return with the least amount of effort and invest behind those top performers. At Kraft Developing Markets, the ten power brands singled out in the 5-10-10 strategy had higher gross margins than other brands in the portfolio, so accelerating their growth almost automatically increased the gross margin for the division overall. What's more, revenues of those ten brands in the developing markets grew at a 17 percent annual rate—much higher than the rest of the business.

But an operation that has gone through the focus process and reached the Virtuous Cycle has to stay agile and continue to execute under the focus principles. Stuff happens—the best-laid plans get disrupted. That's the moment to double down, so to speak—to raise the bets where you get the best bang for your buck. As per Focus7, those are the initiatives that pass muster under the Three Ms (Momentum, Margin, and Materiality). Use the results of those bets to compensate for losses elsewhere.

Whether you are at a small company or a behemoth, this approach can be unnerving, particularly at companies that have a regimented culture. How can you make that $50 million bet? It's not in the budget! But when an aspect of the business is going well—when it has the Three Ms—take advantage to stay ahead of the curve. At various points, Kraft Developing Markets faced shortfalls even after going through Focus7. Two or three markets collapsed. So Kraft invested opportunistically in other markets to make up the losses. That's how the business enjoyed more than twenty quarters of profitable growth.

The trick is to remember the basic principles and move fast. For a large company, maintain the soul of a small company, while leveraging the scale and expertise of size. For a small company, even down to a start-up, leverage the resources that are available outside the company. In both cases, behave like an entrepreneur.

REDUCE COSTS THROUGH EFFICIENCY AND SIMPLIFICATION

Under Focus7, leaders distort resources to back growth initiatives, making trims and cuts and simplifying processes to find the money, people, attention, and effort to support the focus projects. That's a routine that should stay routine—regularly reallocating resources. Even an organization that has gone through Focus7 needs to continue generating fuel by constantly looking for efficiencies.

The war on complexity should never end—after all, complexity never stops creeping. Businesses expand, products proliferate, and support systems mushroom to feed the beast. Sometimes the support systems mushroom even when the business has stalled and is just surviving. Stopping the spread of complexity plays a vital role in the Virtuous Cycle as a significant source of resources.

To keep complexity under control, it helps to pause occasionally and analyze activities with the aim of figuring out where costs pile up and where value is really being added. The best way to do this is with an end-to-end value analysis. That is, you take a product from its point of origin to its purchase by consumers—the so-called end-to-end value chain—and look for waste, complexity, and what makes a difference at each step of the process. You are not just eliminating items, though that certainly can be part of it. The idea is to cut out actions that are unnecessary or that you are just doing because that's the way it's always been done.

At Fonterra, for example, Sanjay was involved in the "Cow to Consumer," an analysis of various dairy products starting with the cow and tracing the value chain through production, transportation, packaging, and finally sales. Fonterra was a relatively low-cost producer—the cow-to-consumer chain was fairly lean. But the company supported 150 or so brands, and infrastructures and procedures had been developed to support all of them. Meantime, only 5 of the brands contributed significantly to Fonterra's growth and profits. Using the value chain as a guide, the company eliminated much of the clutter that surrounded the low-performing brands—considerably simplifying the supply chain. As a result—to use one illustration—a Fonterra salesman making a call wouldn't have to run through a long price list. He was told to concentrate on the focus brands.

The value-chain exercise requires discipline—hard judgments have to be made, and yet it's important not to get too precise in this analysis, because you could easily eat up time. Remember, it's important to get it broadly right, rather than precisely wrong. Do it quickly, come to some fundamental conclusions, and move on.

Kraft Developing Markets ran a successful program called

Project Fuel, which used benchmarking—best in class—to reduce costs, tapping the savings to help fuel growth. A multifunctional team from the field was set up to create a clear road map for all parts of the business to follow. The results were dramatic—so strong in fact that fiercely independent units asked for the team to come in and help. The field team approach contrasts with sending in a platoon of corporate staff, a practice that can feed resentment and often just adds bureaucracy and reporting requirements without improving business results.

Sometimes the effort to cut and simplify arises with striking urgency—another reminder that maintaining the Virtuous Cycle requires agility. Sanjay had a vivid experience of this at the end of 2008. For Kraft Developing Markets, the year was playing out well. The business had undergone Focus7, the numbers were looking good, and the budget for 2009 had been approved. The leadership team planned a dinner in Chicago to share success stories and to celebrate. But by the time the team gathered, Lehman Brothers had gone under and the entire global economy appeared to be teetering on the brink. Nobody knew what would happen, though everyone had read reports from external experts on what was going on in the business. (As it turned out, much of that analysis and the actions suggested turned out to be precisely wrong.)

At the dinner, the conversation turned ominous. Soon enough, the gathered team recognized that the situation was so fluid that analysis would only get the group so far. Finally, Sanjay reiterated his familiar axiom: *Karna Kya Hai?*—*"So what do we do now?"*

In the space of a few hours, the leadership team decided the prudent move would be to cut another 5 percent to 10 percent of the cost base. This was over and above the budget and was termed the "family" target. At the same time, the leaders knew they had to maintain the fundamental strategy, and that meant increasing investments in specific core areas. The group left the dinner that night with the mission to find the cuts, to make them selectively, and to continue to put resources behind the promising bets. Jumping ahead, the net result of that anxious dinner was another strong year for Kraft Developing Markets in the face of a huge global financial crisis.

The leadership pulled it off because they recognized that they were interdependent—they were in this together and had to collaborate for the outcome. They were family. That meant they didn't cut mindlessly across the board, but they went at it strategically, parceling out appropriate targets to each of the functions and countries. The process echoed a growth initiative—local managers were given the targets and told to figure out on their own where to make the cuts based on benchmarking. The entire organization shared the pain, but it also shared expertise. Experts from China advised Brazil. A knowledgeable manager from Chicago went to Mexico. It was peer advising peer, so bruised feelings were avoided for the most part, and in the end everyone enjoyed the resulting success.

IMPROVE GROSS MARGINS THROUGH MIX AND PRODUCTIVITY

The discovery process that kicks off Focus7 should be a constant, albeit in a less structured way. You are looking for two things in particular: products to add that will improve gross margins, and system improvements to raise productivity. Both actions can take a variety of forms.

On the search for improved productivity, the principles of Focus7 should rule—through benchmarking and through ensuring that there is a balance of decision making between global and local levels. One reason companies such as Kraft struggled in their early years in China was that they were applying Western models in a completely different environment. When benchmarked against the local competition, the cost of Kraft's operation was way out of line. The company, for example, had built a plant in China that featured all kinds of unneeded bells and whistles and that was far from reality compared with local competition. Restructuring the China venture raised another question: If you can get a cost profile that's acceptable there, why can't you do it elsewhere?

On today's connected globe, agile companies successfully transfer best practices across markets, increasingly from the developing markets to the developed world. Of course, you need to be careful of quality and safety. Improving productivity is not about cutting corners. It's about finding smart efficiencies, often through the relevant technology. In producing Wheel, for example, Unilever found terrific cost savings by manufacturing the detergent using modified cement mixers instead of far more expensive conventional machines.

GROW REVENUES THROUGH INNOVATION

Higher-margin products, cost cutting, simplification, and productivity improvements generate cash. To complete the Virtuous Cycle, the final step is to invest these resources in innovation that can drive future growth. Business innovation goes far beyond improving a product or introducing a new brand—innovation is a mindset and a culture that needs to permeate the organization. Even focusing on the core represents an innovation for many companies. Every facet of a product is open for improvement. When Kraft bought Cadbury, for example, the Cadbury team in India innovated on positioning (moving chocolate into the generalized sweets market), packaging (creating packages that look like dessert gift boxes), and distribution (doubling in-store displays and doubling the number of temperature-controlled visi coolers to display chocolate in hot summer months).

The Cadbury innovations were spurred by a blank check, and over the years the sense of urgency brought on by a blank-check offer ignited scores of innovations across Kraft Developing Markets. Yet, that sense of urgency should be a constant in every company (albeit, perhaps, at a slightly slower pulse than in a blank-check situation).

The developing markets can be fertile arenas of innovation. The competitive price points are generally lower, the culture brings different perspectives, consumer habits vary, and the market tends to be volatile—a business trying to get a foothold in a developing country has to be flexible and inventive. But those qualities encourage fresh thinking, and the insights gained in one place can often be transferred to another. A standard measure of innovation within a company shows the percentage of sales generated in a year as a result of new products introduced in the last three years. In Kraft Developing Markets, the figure went from 8 percent to 16 percent in five years. Benchmarked against other consumer products companies in developing markets, Kraft ranked among the best in class.

Here's the key point, though, about innovation: It requires focus, too. Manage a few innovative projects well, rather than a lot badly. Too many leaders are innovation junkies, backing changes and new products all across the board. Stay with your core. Follow the principle of starting small, testing, and learning, scaling up only when the potential is clear. Don't introduce a new product unless it has a higher gross margin than the average. Leave those outliers and low performers for another company's portfolio. The business model has to work; it has to be intrinsically profitable. This represents discipline with numbers, and it can be tough in a world that values change as an end in itself. But exceptions to this approach should require approval from the very top.

SECURE THE FUTURE BY INVESTING IN BRANDS AND CUSTOMERS

When you are thinking about growth, think of the difference between bad cholesterol and good cholesterol. Growth that gives a temporary spike to results can be like bad cholesterol, damaging the system over the long term, often by cheapening the brand. But growth that builds on itself is like good cholesterol, improving health over the long term. That doesn't mean you have to wait forever to enjoy good results. In the developing markets sphere, for example, some people have argued that you need to wait ten years or so to make money. Baloney. What you need is a good business model and an appropriate portfolio.

But to keep the profits rolling in, it's not sufficient to produce a lean operation—you've also got to invest in advertising and in promoting your focus brands, building them for the future. And you've got to invest in making the product available—opening the appropriate channels to make sure that what you are selling is in the right place at the right time. That's another aspect of a refrain you've heard often in these pages: Look out the window, not in the mirror.

These days, of course, one of the favorite channels is online. As in any new market, you've got to start with a business model that works, focusing on where you can win. Best Buy Co., Inc. (where Sanjay sits on the board), is the largest consumer electronics retailer in the world, essentially because of its strength in North America. Recently, Best Buy has initiated a major investment in online business, building on its advantage in the huge network of stores spread around the country, many within a short distance of millions of consumers. For its online initiative, the company is leveraging that network, which allows for quicker shipping and lower costs.

Winning companies take a farsighted approach to building their business. They avoid one-shots. They concentrate on robust ideas, with points of difference, building Brands with Soul.

There's a reason we speak of the Virtuous *Cycle*. Each of the elements feeds on the others and in turn pushes the process forward. With the right elements in place, the spiral should keep growing.

While the growth journey never ends, we have come to the end of our story in this book. We hope that you have enjoyed walking with us through the steps of Focus7—a framework that is designed to get your business to the endgame of profitable growth that sustains itself. Over the years, Sanjay nurtured and refined the ideas that would become Focus7 while applying them on the front lines of companies around the globe. Through research and consulting, Mohan uncovered many of the same principles while working for a far-ranging roster of businesses. The two of us started sharing our insights and experiences while playing golf together on the lovely Harborside golf course on the south end of Chicago, and those conversations led to this book.

Though some of what we say here contradicts conventional wisdom, nothing is particularly complicated. That's one of the points of our framework: Stick to the essentials. The words we keep using—focus, core, simplicity, clarity, candor—form the basis of common sense and lucid communication. And those qualities are at the heart of Focus7.

Building a business is almost never easy, and the process rarely graphs as a straight line. Setbacks are part of the game, and, as we've said, what's important is to learn from them. But running a business—even a piece of a business—should be an exhilarating, rewarding experience. We hope Focus7 provides the advice to bring you to Fewer, Bigger, Bolder bets—and the joy of winning.

INDEX